PRESIDENT KIMBALL SPEAKS OUT

PRESIDENT KIMBALL SPEAKS OUT

President Spencer W. Kimball

Deseret Book Company
Salt Lake City, Utah
1981

©1981 Deseret Book Company
All rights reserved
Printed in the United States of America
First printing September 1981

Library of Congress Catalog Card No. 81-68861
ISBN 0-87747-881-3

CONTENTS

PRESIDENT KIMBALL
SPEAKS OUT ON:

PRESIDENT KIMBALL
SPEAKS OUT ON
MORALITY

My beloved young people, while this is a grave responsibility, and not an easy one, I am eager to discuss with you some matters of importance.

I love youth. I rejoice when they grow up clean and stalwart and tall. I sorrow with them when they have misfortunes and remorse and troubles.

Numerous disasters have occurred in mid-ocean by collisions of ships, sometimes with icebergs, and numerous people have gone to watery graves. I believe you young people are wholesome and basically good and sound; but you, too, are traveling oceans that to you are at least partially uncharted, where there are shoals and rocks and icebergs and other vessels, and where great disasters can come unless warnings are heeded.

1

A couple of years ago as my jet plane soared in the air gaining altitude, the voice of the stewardess came clearly over the loudspeaker: "We are moving into a storm area. We shall skirt the danger, but there may be some turbulence. Be sure your seat belts are securely fastened."

And, as a leader of the Church and in a measure being responsible for youth and their well-being, I raise my voice to say to you: "You are in a hazardous area and period. Tighten your belts, hold on, and you can survive the turbulence."

I have interviewed thousands of young people, and many seem to flounder. Some give excuses for their errors and indulge in unwarranted rationalizations. I hope I may be able to clarify at least in some areas the stand of the God of heaven and his church on some vital issues.

First, let us pause to remind ourselves that we are the spiritual children of God, and that we are his supreme creation. In each of us there is the potentiality to become a God—pure, holy, true, influential, powerful, independent of earthly forces. We learn from the scriptures that we each have eternal existence, that we were in the beginning with God. (See Abraham 3:22.) That understanding gives to us a unique sense of man's dignity.

Further, it is the destiny of men and women to join together to make eternal family units. In the context of lawful marriage, the intimacy of sexual relations is right and divinely approved. There is nothing unholy or degrading about sexuality in itself, for by that means men and women join in a process of creation and in an expression of love.

2

But there are false teachers everywhere, using speech and pornographic literature, magazines, radio, TV, street talk—spreading damnable heresies which break down moral standards, and this to gratify the lust of the flesh.

Lucifer in his diabolical scheming deceives the unwary and uses every tool at his command. Seldom does one go to a convention, a club meeting, a party, or a social gathering without hearing vulgarity, obscenity, and suggestive stories, degrading to marriage and the sacred power of procreation.

Peter cautioned us: "Be sober, be vigilant; because your adversary the devil, as a roaring lion, walketh about, seeking whom he may devour." (1 Peter 5:8.)

And the Savior said that the very elect would be deceived by Lucifer if it were possible. Lucifer will use his logic to confuse and his rationalizations to destroy. He will shade meanings, open doors an inch at a time, and lead from purest white through all the shades of gray to the darkest black.

So I wish to help define meanings of words and acts for you young people, to fortify you against error, anguish, pain, and sorrow.

Necking, Petting, Fornication

I will begin with a true story. The characters are real.

He was well-proportioned and, like King David, "ruddy, and withal of a beautiful countenance, and goodly to look to." (1 Samuel 16:12.)

With him at his side was a lovely girl, slight of

3

frame and beautiful of face and form. It was obvious that they loved one another, for as they sat together across the desk from me, he reached quietly for her hand and there were meaningful glances.

The melodious voice was hesitant and a bit choked with emotion as he introduced his girl friend, and there was pleading in their eyes. "We are in difficulty, Brother Kimball," he said. "We have broken the law of chastity. We prayed and fasted and agonized and finally came to the conclusion that we must try to make adjustments.

"That junior prom date was a turning point. It started out a very special date. But as I see it now, it turned out to be a tragic one, the beginning of our troubles. When I saw her coming downstairs that night, I thought no girl was ever so beautiful and so sweet. We danced through the evening; and then when we sat in the car, long and silently afterward, my thoughts became unruly as we became more and more intimate.

"Neither of us dreamed what was happening to us," he continued, "but all the elements were there to break down resistance. We did not notice time—the hours passed. The simple kisses we had often exchanged gradually developed into petting. We stopped at that. But there were other nights—the bars were down. We loved each other so much that we convinced ourselves that it was not so wrong merely to pet, since we sort of belonged to one another anyway. Where we ended one night became the starting point for the next night, and we continued on and on, until finally it happened—almost as though we could not con-

4

trol ourselves—we had intercourse. We had even talked about it and agreed that whatever else we did, we would not go that far. And then when it was late—so late, so everlastingly late—we woke up to the meaning of what we had done."

Immorality does not begin in adultery or perversion. It begins with little indiscretions like sex thoughts, sex discussions, passionate kissing, petting, and such, growing with every exercise. The small indiscretion seems powerless compared to the sturdy body, the strong mind, the sweet spirit of youth who give way to the first temptation. But soon the strong has become weak, the master the slave, spiritual growth curtailed. But if the first unrighteous act is never given root, the tree will grow to beautiful maturity, and the youthful life will grow toward God, our Father.

"Can we be forgiven, Brother Kimball?" the young couple asked.

"Yes," I replied, "the Lord and his church can and will forgive, but not easily. The way of the transgressor is hard. It always has been and it always will be. The Lord said: 'I tell thee, thou shalt not depart thence, till thou hast paid the very last mite.' " (Luke 12:59.)

I went on to tell them that in his goodness he provided for us a way to forgiveness. One may do as he pleases, but he cannot evade responsibility. He may break laws, but he cannot avoid penalties. One gets by with nothing. God is just. Paul said, "Be not deceived; God is not mocked; for whatsoever a man soweth, that shall he also reap." (Galatians 6:7.)

5

Serious as is the sin of fornication (sexual intercourse by the unmarried), there is forgiveness upon condition of total repentance. But first, one must come to a realization of the seriousness of his sin. Since the beginning there has been in the world a wide range of sins. Many of them involve harm to others, but every sin is against ourselves and God, for sins limit our progress, curtail our development, and estrange us from good people, good influences, and from our Lord.

The early apostles and prophets mention numerous sins that are reprehensible. Many of them are sexual sins—adultery, being without natural affection, lustfulness, infidelity, incontinence, filthy communications, impurity, inordinate affection, fornication. They include all sexual relations outside marriage—petting, sex perversion, masturbation, and preoccupation with sex in one's thoughts and talking. Included are every hidden and secret sin and all unholy and impure thoughts and practices. One of the worst of these is incest. The dictionary defines incest as "sexual intercourse between persons so closely related that they are forbidden by law to marry." The spirituality of one's life may be severely, and sometimes irreparably, damaged by such an ugly sin. The First Presidency and the Quorum of the Twelve have determined that the penalty for incest shall be excommunication. Also, one excommunicated for incest shall not be baptized again into the Church without the written permission of the First Presidency.

Conscience tells the individual when he is entering forbidden worlds, and it continues to prick until silenced by the will or by sin's repetition.

Can anyone truthfully say he did not know such things were wrong? These unholy practices, whatever may be their unmentionable names with all their approaches and numerous manifestations, are condemned by the Lord and his church. Some may be more heinous than others, but all are sin, in spite of statements to the contrary of those who falsely pretend to know. The Lord's prophets declare they are not right.

The world may have its norm; the Church has a different one. It may be considered normal by the people of the world to use tobacco; the Church's standard is a higher plane where smoking is not done. The world's norm may permit men and women social drinking; the Lord's church lifts its people to a norm of total abstinence. The world may countenance premarital sex experiences, but the Lord and his church condemn in no uncertain terms any and every sex relationship outside of marriage.

Paul lashed out against these unholy evidences of the vulgar mind and of uncontrolled passion and desire: "Wherefore God also gave them up to uncleanness through the lusts of their own hearts, to dishonour their own bodies between themselves." (Romans 1:24.)

Since courtship is prelude to marriage and encourages close associations, many have convinced themselves that intimacies are legitimate —a part of the courting process. Many have cast off bridle and harness and have relaxed the restraints. Instead of remaining in the field of simple expressions of affection, some have turned themselves loose to "necking," with its intimate contacts and its passionate kissing. Necking is the younger member of this unholy family. Its bigger sister is called "petting, with fondling of the private parts of the body for the purpose of sexual arousal." When the intimacies have reached this stage, they are surely the sins condemned by the Savior:

"Ye have heard that it was said by them of old time, Thou shalt not commit adultery:

"But I say unto you, That whosoever looketh on a woman to lust after her hath committed adultery with her already in his heart." (Matthew 5:27-28.)

Who would say that he or she who pets has not become lustful, has not become passionate? Is it not this most abominable practice that God rebuked in his modern reiteration of the Ten Commandments: "Thou shalt not steal; neither commit adultery, nor kill, nor do anything like unto it"? (D&C 59:6.)

What, may I ask you, is like unto adultery if it is not petting? Did not the Lord recognize that this heinous sin is but the devil's softening process for the final acts of adultery or fornication? Can a person, in the light of the Lord's scriptures, pursue the path of petting with clear conscience? Can anyone convince himself that this is not deep sin?

We must repeat what we have said many times: Fornication with all its big and little brothers and sisters was evil and wholly condemned by the Lord in Adam's day, in Moses' day, in Paul's day, and in our own day. The Church has no tolerance for any kind of perversions. The Lord has indicated his lack of tolerance, stating: "For I the Lord cannot look upon sin with the least degree of allowance." (D&C 1:31.)

I believe the youth of Zion want to hear the clear and unmistakable tones of the trumpet, and it is my hope that I can play the tune with accuracy and precision so that no honest person will ever be confused. I hope fervently that I am making clear the position of the Lord and his church on these unmentionable practices.

When the scriptures are so plain, how can anyone justify immoralities and call them love? Is black white? Is evil good? Is purity filthiness?

That the Church's stand on morality may be understood, we declare firmly and unalterably that it is not an outworn garment, faded, old-fashioned, and threadbare. God is the same yesterday, today, and forever, and his covenants and doctrines are immutable. And when the sun grows cold and the stars no longer shine, the law of chastity will still be basic in God's world and in the Lord's church. Old values are upheld by the Church not because they are old, but rather because they are right.

I would add a suggestion for avoiding undue temptation. Young men and women, not yet ready for marriage, should be friends with many others, but they should not engage in courting. Immaturity makes them susceptible to temptation. We want them to grow up clean, with a life plan for missions, then wholesome courting and eternal marriage in the holy temple. It is timing that is vital. The sexual relationship that is wrong before marriage is right and beautiful as part of the union encouraged by God. Friendship, not courtship, should be the relationship of teen-agers.

Self-abuse and Homosexuality

Masturbation, a rather common indiscretion, is not approved of the Lord nor of his church, regardless of what may be said by others whose "norms" are lower. Latter-day Saints are urged to avoid this practice. Anyone fettered by this weakness should abandon the habit before he goes on a mission or receives the holy priesthood or goes in the temple for his blessings.

Sometimes masturbation is the introduction to the more serious sin of exhibitionism and the gross sin of homosexuality. We would avoid mentioning these unholy terms and these reprehensible practices were it not for the fact that we have a responsibility to the youth of Zion that they be not deceived by those who would call bad good, and black white.

The unholy transgression of homosexuality is either rapidly growing or tolerance is giving it wider publicity. If one has such desires and tendencies, he overcomes them the same as if he had the urge toward petting or fornication or adultery. The Lord condemns and forbids this practice with a vigor equal to his condemnation of adultery and other such sex acts. And the Church will excommunicate as readily any unrepentant addict.

Again, contrary to the belief and statements of many people, this sin, like fornication, may be overcome and may be forgiven, but only upon deep and abiding repentance, which means total abandonment and complete transformation of thought and act. The fact that some governments and some churches and numerous corrupted individuals have tried to reduce such behavior from criminal offense to personal privilege does not change the nature nor the seriousness of the practice. Good men, wise men, God-fearing men everywhere still denounce the practice as being unworthy of sons and daughters of God; and Christ's church denounces it and condemns it so long as men have bodies that can be defiled.

James said: "A double minded man is unstable in all his ways. . . .

"Blessed is the man that endureth temptation: for when he is tried, he shall receive the crown of life, which the Lord hath promised to them that love him.

"Let no man say when he is tempted, I am tempted of God: for God cannot be tempted with evil, neither tempteth he any man:

"But every man is tempted, when he is drawn away of his own lust, and enticed.

"Then when lust hath conceived, it bringeth forth sin: and sin, when it is finished, bringeth forth death.

"Do not err, my beloved brethren." (James 1:8, 12-16.)

This heinous homosexual sin is of the ages. Many cities and civilizations have gone out of existence because of it. It was present in Israel's wandering days, tolerated by the Greeks, and found in the baths of corrupt Rome.

This is a most unpleasant subject to dwell upon, but I am pressed to speak of it boldly so that no youth in the Church will ever have any question in his mind as to the illicit and diabolical nature of this perverse program. Again, Lucifer deceives and prompts logic and rationalization that will destroy men and make them servants of Satan forever. Paul told Timothy: "For the time will come when they will not endure sound doctrine; but after their own lusts shall they heap to themselves teachers, having itching ears; And they shall turn away their ears from the truth, and shall be turned unto fables." (2 Timothy 4:3-4. See also Moses 5:50-55.)

"God made me that way," some say, as they rationalize and excuse themselves for their perversions. "I can't help it," they add. This is blasphemy. Is man not made in the image of God, and does he think God to be "that way"? Man is responsible for his own sins. It is possible that he may rationalize and excuse himself until the groove is so deep that he cannot get out without great difficulty, but he can resist, he can change. Temptations come to all people. The difference between the reprobate and the worthy person is generally that one yielded and the other resisted. It is true that one's background may make the decision and accomplishment easier or more difficult, but if one is mentally alert, he can still control his future. That is the gospel message—personal responsibility.

And now, my dear young people, I have spoken frankly and boldly against the sins of the day. Even though I dislike such a subject, I believe it necessary to warn the youth against the onslaught of the arch tempter who, with his army of emissaries and all the tools at his command, would destroy all the youth of Zion, largely through deception, misrepresentation, and lies.

"Be wise in the days of your probation," said Mormon; "strip yourselves of all uncleanness; ask not, that ye may consume it on your lusts, but ask with a firmness unshaken, that ye will yield to no temptation, but that ye will serve the true and living God." (Mormon 9:28.)

Repentance

Beloved youth, for those of you who have erred, the Lord and his church can forgive. The image of a loving, forgiving God comes through clearly to those who read and understand the scriptures. Since he is our Father, he naturally desires to raise us up, not to push us down; to help us live, not to bring about our spiritual death.

Repentance seems to fall into five steps:

1. *Sorrow for sin.* To be sorry for our sin, we must know something of its serious implications. When fully convicted, we condition our minds to follow such processes as will rid us of the effects of the sin. We are sorry. We are willing to make amends, to pay penalties, to suffer even to excommunication if necessary.

2. *Abandonment of sin.* It is best when one discontinues his error because of his realization of the gravity of his sin and is willing to comply with the laws of God. The thief may abandon his evil in prison, but true repentance would have him forsake it before his arrest and return his booty

without enforcement. The sex offender who voluntarily ceases his unholy practices is headed toward forgiveness.

Alma said, "Blessed are they who humble themselves without being compelled to be humble." (Alma 32:16.)

The discontinuance must be a permanent one. True repentance does not permit repetition. The Lord revealed this to the Prophet Joseph Smith concerning repentance: "By this ye may know if a man repenteth of his sins—behold, he will confess them and forsake them." (D&C 58:43.)

3. *Confession of sin.* The confession of sin is an important element in repentance. Many offenders have seemed to feel that a few prayers to the Lord were sufficient. They have thus justified themselves in hiding their sins. "He that covereth his sins shall not prosper: but whoso confesseth and forsaketh them shall have mercy." (Proverbs 28:13.)

Especially grave errors such as sexual sins shall be confessed to the bishop as well as to the Lord. There are two remissions one might wish to have: first, the forgiveness from the Lord, and second, the forgiveness of the Lord's church through its leaders.

As soon as one has an inner conviction of his sins, he should go to the Lord in "mighty prayer" as did Enos, and never cease his supplications until he shall, like Enos, receive the assurance that his sins have been forgiven by the Lord. It is unthinkable that God absolves serious sins upon a few requests. He is likely to wait until there has been long, sustained repentance, as evidenced by

a willingness to comply with all His other requirements.

Next, the offender should seek the forgiveness
of the Church through his bishop. No priest nor
elder is authorized to thus act for the Church. The
Lord has a consistent, orderly plan. Every soul
who lives in a stake is given a bishop who, by the
very order of his calling and his ordination, is a
"judge in Israel." Where the stakes are not organized, the branch president functions in the
bishop's role. The bishop is our best earthly
friend. He will hear the problems, judge the
seriousness, then determine the degree of repentance and decide if it warrants an eventual forgiveness. He does this as the earthly representative of God—the master physician, the master
psychologist, the master psychiatrist. If repentance is sufficient he may waive penalties, which
is tantamount to forgiveness. The bishop claims
no authority to absolve sins, but he does share the
burden, waive penalties, and relieve tension and
strain; he may also assure a continuance of activity. He will keep the whole matter most confiden-
tial.

4. *Restitution for sin.* When one is humble in
sorrow, has unconditionally abandoned the evil,
and has confessed to those assigned by the Lord,
he should next restore insofar as possible that
which was damaged. If he burglarized, he should
return to the rightful owner that which was sto-
len. Perhaps one reason murder is unforgivable is
that having taken a life, the murderer cannot restore it; restitution in full is not possible. Also, one
who has robbed of virtue cannot give it back.

However, the truly repentant soul will usually find things that can be done to restore to some extent. The true spirit of repentance demands this. Ezekiel taught, "If the wicked . . . give again that he had robbed, walk in the statutes of life, without committing iniquity; he shall surely live." (Ezekiel 33:15.) Moses taught, "If a man shall steal an ox or a sheep, . . . he shall restore five oxen for an ox, and four sheep for a sheep." (Exodus 22:1.)

A pleading sinner must also forgive all people of all offenses committed against himself. The Lord is under no obligation to forgive us unless our hearts are fully purged of all hate, bitterness, and accusations against all others.

5. *Do the will of the Father.* I received many birthday cards for my eighty-third birthday in March of 1978. One was bound in a book and had 4,700 autographs of youths who had signed the book. They were pledging their lives with such statements as the following:

"I pledge to you and the Lord to lengthen my stride, to quicken my pace, to stretch my soul in the work of the Lord.

"I promise to pay my tithing faithfully and regularly all my life."

"I promise to you and the Lord that I will live the Word of Wisdom, even though temptations arise. I will never touch tobacco, liquor, tea, coffee, or drugs."

"I promise to remember my nightly and morning prayers. I shall never forget the Lord nor his rich promises, his protecting care, and his rich blessings."

"I promise that I will keep my life clean and

unspotted from the numerous insidious temptations. There will never be any approach to immorality of any nature."

"I pledge that I shall lengthen my stride in the reading and absorbing of the scriptures and other good books."

"I pledge sincerely that I will quicken my pace in my love of my fellowmen and work together with them in achieving righteousness."

"I will stretch my soul to understand all of the commandments of the Lord and live them with great precision and care and love."

Now, brothers and sisters, you are sweet and wonderful, and we are proud of you, proud of the records you make, proud of the devotion you show, proud of the sacrifice you make. I tell you, we love you. How we pray for you every meeting we hold, every night and morning in our homes, and every night in our bedrooms; we pray for you that you will keep yourselves clean and free from all the ugly things the world is pushing upon us, the drugs and drinking and smoking, the vulgarity, the pornography—all those things that are destructive. You must not give yourselves to them.

Put on the full armor of God. Attend to your personal and family prayers and family devotions; keep holy the Sabbath; live strictly the Word of Wisdom; attend to all family duties; and above all, keep your life clean and free from all unholy and impure thoughts and actions. Avoid all associations that degrade and lower the high, righteous standards set up for us. Then your life will sail smoothly, and peace and joy will surround you.

PRESIDENT KIMBALL
SPEAKS OUT ON
TESTIMONY

I n a high council testimony meeting some
time ago I heard one of the number say, "I
am happy in the work and have made research,
and this church and its doctrines satisfy me better
than anything I have found." Then another arose
and with deep feeling declared, "This is the work
of God. I *know* it. It is the Lord's eternal plan of exaltation. I *know* that Jesus lives and is the Redeemer." I was uplifted by his sureness. And I
went to the revelations of the Lord to see how it is
that some are so sure while others are passive or
have doubts.

I recall the experience of the apostles when the
Lord manifested himself to them after his resurrection. Jesus found a group who accepted him,

but one of the quorum who was absent declared that he would not believe unless he could see in the Lord's hands the print of the nails and thrust his hand into the wounded side. And the Savior, anticipating Thomas's doubt, commanded him to thrust forth his hand and feel and know; then he said, "Thomas, because thou hast seen me, thou hast believed: blessed are they that have not seen, and yet have believed." (John 20:29.)

Peter was asked by the Savior, "But whom say ye that I am?" And Peter, speaking for his brethren, the other apostles, replied, "Thou art the Christ, the Son of the living God." The Savior's next remark is a most significant one. He said, "Blessed art thou, Simon Barjona: for flesh and blood hath not revealed it unto thee, but my Father which is in heaven." (Matthew 16:13-17.)

Who revealed this startling truth to Peter? Our Father in heaven. How did he do it? By revelation. This basic knowledge that Jesus is the Christ, the Redeemer, the Savior, came not from any man or from any book or from any college. Peter received it directly from our Heavenly Father through the ministrations of the Holy Ghost.

God cannot be found through research alone, nor his gospel understood and appreciated by study only, for no one may know the Father or the Son but "he to whom the Son will reveal him." (Luke 10:22.) The skeptic will someday either in time or eternity learn to his sorrow that his egotism has robbed him of much joy and growth; that has been decreed by the Lord. The things of God cannot be understood by the spirit of man; man cannot by himself find out God or his program, and no amount of scientific or philosophical research or rationalizing will bring a testimony. It must come through the heart when compliance with the program has made the person eligible to receive that reward.

In the last chapter of the Book of Mormon we read this: "And when ye shall receive these things, I would exhort you that ye would ask God, the Eternal Father, in the name of Christ, if these things are not true; and if ye shall ask with a sincere heart, with real intent, having faith in Christ, he will manifest the truth of it unto you, by the power of the Holy Ghost." (Moroni 10:4.)

Ask for Revelation

The Lord has reiterated his promise with much emphasis: "If thou shalt ask, thou shalt receive revelation upon revelation, knowledge upon knowledge, that thou mayest know the mysteries and peaceable things—that which bringeth joy, that which bringeth life eternal. . . . For unto you it is given to know the mysteries of the kingdom, but unto the world it is not given to know them." (D&C 42:61, 65.)

That is no casual promise. It is a positive one, and every soul in this world may have a revelation, the same revelation that Peter had. That revelation will be a testimony, a knowledge that Christ lives, that Jesus Christ is the Redeemer of this world. Every soul may have this assurance, and when he gets this testimony, it will come from God, and not from study alone.

When you individually know that Jesus was

not only a great philosopher but that he was also verily the Son of God, that he came into the world in the way that we claim he did, and that he went out of the world for the purpose that we claim he did—when you know that positively, and know that Joseph Smith was a prophet of God, and that this is the divine church established by Jesus Christ, then you have had a revelation. Treasure it as Mary did the revelation that came to her when she was told that she was to be the mother of the Son of God. She treasured it in her heart.

Live the Commandments

The Redeemer declared: "My doctrine is not mine, but his that sent me. If any man will do his will, he shall know of the doctrine, whether it be of God, or whether I speak of myself." (John 7:16-17.)

What is it to *know* of the doctrine? It is an unwavering assurance. The Lord has offered a rich reward but has provided that it can be had only by meeting certain requirements. In this case the blessing promised is a *knowledge of the divinity of the doctrine.* And in this case the law or requirement is that one must "do his will." Most of us know what his will is, far more than we have disposition or ability to comply.

One must not only be baptized and receive the Holy Ghost, but also live the commandments to be given the knowledge of the divinity of the work. Mere passive acceptance of the doctrines will not give the testimony; no casual half-compliance with the program will bring that assu-

21

rance; it will come only through an all-out effort to live his commandments.

A man once said to me, "I assiduously avoid all testimony meetings. I can't take the sentimental and emotional statements that some of the people make. I can't accept these doctrines unless I can in an intellectual and rational way prove every step." I knew this type of man, as I have met others like him. In no case have they gone all-out to live the commandments: little or no tithing, only occasional attendance at meetings, considerable criticism of the doctrines, the organizations, and the leaders, and we know well why they could have no testimony. Remember that the Lord said: "I, the Lord, am bound when ye do what I say; but when ye do not what I say, ye have no promise." (D&C 82:10.) Such people have failed to "do what he says," so of course, they have no promise.

Bear Witness to One Another

Testimony meetings are some of the best meetings in the ward in the whole month, if you have the spirit. If you are bored at a testimony meeting, there is something the matter with *you*, and not with others. You can get up and bear your testimony and you'll think it is the best meeting in the month; but if you sit there and count the grammatical errors and laugh at the man who can't speak very well, you'll be bored, and on that "board" you'll slip right out of the Kingdom. Don't forget it! You have to *fight* for a testimony. You have to *keep* fighting!

The Lord says in section 60 of the Doctrine and

Covenants, "With some I am not well pleased, for they will not open their mouths." (D&C 60:2.) What does he mean? He says that if they do not use it, they will lose what he has given them. They lose their spirit. They lose their testimony. And this priceless thing that you have can slip right out of your life.

Every month the First Presidency and the Twelve meet with all the General Authorities in the temple. They bear testimony and tell each other how they love one another just as they love all of you. Why do the General Authorities need a testimony meeting? For the same reason that you need a testimony meeting. Do you think that you can go three, six, nine, or even twelve months without bearing your testimony, and still keep its full value?

Some of our good people get so terrified of triteness that they try to steer around and away from their testimonies by getting out on the fringes. Don't you ever worry about triteness in testimony. When the President of the Church bears his testimony, he says, "I know that Joseph Smith was called of God, a divine representative. I know that Jesus is the Christ, the Son of the living God." You see, it is the same thing every one of you says. That is a testimony. It never gets old, never gets old! Tell the Lord frequently how much you love him.

A testimony is not an exhortation; it is not a sermon (none of you are here to exhort the rest); it is not a travelogue. You are there to bear your own witness. It is amazing what you can say in sixty seconds by way of testimony, or 120 seconds, or

240, or whatever time you are given, if you confine yourselves to testimony. We'd like to know how you feel. Do you love the work, really? Are you happy in your work? Do you love the Lord? Are you glad that you are a member of the Church?

Testimony is a tremendous thing, a most important thing. Any minister or priest can quote scripture and present dialogues, but not every priest or minister can bear his testimony. Don't you sit there in your fast meeting and cheat yourself and say, "I guess I won't bear my testimony today. I guess that wouldn't be fair to the other members, because I have had so many opportunities." You bear your testimony. And one minute is long enough to bear it.

You have a testimony! It needs building and lifting and enlarging, of course, and that is what you are doing. Every time you bear your testimony, it becomes strengthened. I ask missionaries, "What think ye of Christ and the claims that are made?" And I hear inspiring testimonies from youth—sure testimonies, ringing with conviction. I am gratified at the replies saying, "He is the Christ, the Son of the living God."

Almost without exception the missionaries have studied, prayed, kept the commandments, and borne their testimonies, and they have been rewarded with a knowledge as promised by their Savior, in proportion to their faithfulness. It is not blind loyalty, but faithful observance and turning of keys that open the storehouse of spiritual knowledge. The Lord will not discriminate between his children, but he delights to own and bless us all, if we will let him.

The Savior could have taken highly trained minds from the temple porches for the chief builders of his kingdom, but he went to the seashore to get humble fishermen. He wanted men who would not depend upon their own intellects only to ferret out the truths; rather, he sought unbiased men to whom he might reveal his new program, men who were trusting and sincere and willing to serve. They lived the truth, and they *knew* the truth, and the truth made them free and gave them peace.

To emphasize the spiritual dimension is not to reject the study of scriptures and the doctrines. The scriptures testify of Christ. Study is an important element, of course, but there must be much prayer and reaching associated with study, and then revelation comes.

The Vanity of Skepticism

To acquire a testimony, then, one must be in tune with the Spirit of the Lord, keep his commandments, and be sincere. To say that another person cannot see the light because you fail to comprehend it is to place unwarranted limitations on another's power. To say that no one can know of the doctrine because you do not know is like saying that there is no germ or virus because it is not visible to you.

"If in this life only we have hope in Christ, we are of all men most miserable." (2 Corinthians 15:19.) There are many miserable people in the world because they have no hope. But when the gospel lights a life, then hope comes into it, and the person is given something for which to live. Study, if you will, the philosophies of men, which continue to change, but remember to appraise and evaluate such theories as human in origin. Anchor your faith, your hopes, and your future to God, who is unchangeable, for he is the same yesterday, today, and forever. If you cannot understand fully today, wait patiently and truth will unfold and light will come. Accept unreservedly the fact that God lives, that Jesus is the Christ, and that the kind of life we live here will determine the degree of eternal joy and peace we shall have throughout eternity.

Sometimes people let their hearts get so set upon things and the honors of this world that they cannot learn the lessons they most need to learn. Simple truths are often rejected in favor of the much less demanding philosophies of men.

The Lord will bless us and watch over us, sometimes dramatically. At other times, he will leave us to cope with the challenge rather than removing or diverting the challenge. He will not let us be tried beyond that which we can bear, but he will choose to push us at times. We can expect to be tested. Moroni wrote: "Dispute not because ye see not, for ye receive no witness until after the trial of your faith." (Ether 12:6.)

My Witness

I know without question that God lives, and I have a feeling of sorrow for those people in the world who live in the gray area of doubt, who do not have such an assurance.

I know that the Lord Jesus Christ is the Only Begotten Son of our Heavenly Father, and that he assisted in the creation of man and all that serves man, including the earth and all that is in the world. He was the Redeemer of mankind, the Savior of this world, and the author of the plan of salvation for all men and the exaltation of all who live the laws he has given.

He it was who organized this vehicle—this true church—and called it after his name: The Church of Jesus Christ of Latter-day Saints. In it are all the saving graces.

I know that the Lord has contact with his prophets, and that he reveals the truth today to his servants as he did in the days of Adam and Abraham and Moses and Peter and Joseph and the numerous others throughout time. The countless testimonies of the Brethren throughout the ages are positive and uniform, uplifting and faith-building and hope-building, and they encourage worthiness. God's messages of light and truth are as surely given to man today as in any other dispensation.

I know this is true, and I bear this testimony to you, my beloved brothers and sisters and friends in all the world.

PRESIDENT KIMBALL
SPEAKS OUT ON
BEING A MISSIONARY

The gathering of Israel is now in progress. Hundreds of thousands of people have been baptized into the Church. Millions more will join the Church. And this is the way we will gather Israel. It is to be done by missionary work. It is your responsibility to attend to this missionary work, and we hope you will not excuse yourselves from this responsibility.

The gospel knows no nationality. All people in the world are the sons and daughters of God. They are all our brothers and sisters. And we are anxious to fulfill the obligation of the Lord Jesus Christ when he gave us that basic command, "Go ye into all the world, and preach the gospel to every creature." (Mark 16:15.)

Who Should Go on a Mission?

I have been asked, "Should every young man who is a member of the Church fill a mission?" And I respond with the answer the Lord has given: Yes, every worthy man should fill a mission. The Lord expects it of him. And if he is not now worthy to fill a mission, then he should start at once to qualify himself. The Lord has instructed, "Send forth the elders of my church unto the nations which are afar off; unto the islands of the sea; send forth unto foreign lands; call upon all nations, first upon the Gentiles, and then upon the Jews." (D&C 133:8.)

Thus, the elders—the young men of the Church of the age to be ordained elders—should be prepared and eager to fill a mission for the Church throughout the world. Presently, only about one-third of the eligible young men of the Church are serving full-time missions! One-third is not "every young man." Stakes typically range between 25 percent and 40 percent of their eligible young men on missions. That's all! Where are the other young men? Why do they not go on missions?

Certainly every male member of the Church *should* fill a mission, like he *should* pay his tithing, like he *should* attend his meetings, like he *should* keep his life clean and free from the ugliness of the world and plan a celestial marriage in the temple of the Lord.

While there is no compulsion for him to do any of these things, he should do them because they are right.

Someone might also ask, "Should every

young woman, should every father and mother, should every member of the Church serve a mission?" Again, the Lord has given the answer: Yes, every man, woman, and child—every young person and every little boy and girl—should serve a mission. This does not mean that they must serve abroad or even be formally called and set apart as full-time missionaries. But it does mean that each of us is responsible to bear witness of the gospel truths that we have been given. We all have relatives, neighbors, friends, and fellow workmen, and it is our responsibility to pass the truths of the gospel on to them, by example as well as by precept.

In addition, many young women have a desire to serve a full-time mission, and they are also welcome in the Lord's service. This responsibility is not on them as it is on the elders, but they will receive rich blessings for their unselfish sacrifice. The Lord is pleased at their willingness to bring souls to him.

What a thrilling thing it is, my dear brothers and sisters who are fellow members of the kingdom of God, to be entrusted by the Lord to serve as messengers of his word to our brothers and sisters who are not members of the Church. The scriptures are abundantly clear in stating that all members of the Church are responsible to do missionary work: "It becometh every man who hath been warned to warn his neighbor." (D&C 88:81.)

We who are leaders should not be afraid to ask our youth to render service to their fellowmen or to sacrifice for the kingdom. Our youth have a sense of intrinsic idealism, and we need have no fear in appealing to that idealism when we call them to serve.

One young man spoke tellingly of this when he recently said, "I hope that when I am called to go on a full-time mission, I am *called* and *told* that the Lord wants me to go, and that it is my *duty*, rather than just being told that a mission would be a good thing for me if I wanted to go."

All young men in the Church should be very eager to go on a mission, and they should also help their parents to fill missions after the families are raised. Young people should study the gospel, prepare themselves for service in the Church, and keep the commandments as diligently as it is possible to do.

Young people who have planned to fill missions are more fruitful, more effective, and more successful when they serve, and more people will come into the Church and will create more enthusiasm, and there will be a chain reaction. Is there any other thing than the gospel that would have a greater chain reaction and affect more interests and people?

Learning in Seminary and Institute Classes

Can you imagine what would happen to the seminary and institute programs if they were populated with wonderful young people who have been planning for missions from birth until seminary days? Seminary and institute buildings would be crowded with a new kind of maturity and seriousness that would give the Church a new image. The morality of the youth would greatly increase. They would be taught cleanliness and righteousness in a way that they have never been taught before. Can you see what would happen to sacrament meeting attendance and other church activity?

I wish every young man and young woman could go to seminary, because that is where they learn many of the truths of the gospel. Seminary is where many of them get their ideals settled in their minds about what they are going to do, and they go on missions.

It is incumbent upon all young people to prepare themselves for the solemn obligation and privilege of missionary work. As they learn the alphabet, the times tables, and later things requisite to their college work, they will be preparing for their life's work. In the same manner they should be preparing all the days of their childhood and youth for the great mission of their young adulthood and their life's spiritual growth.

Preparation in Three Areas

Missionary preparation consists largely of effort in three areas:

1. Keeping one's life clean and worthy and remaining free from all sins of the world. The Lord has provided that forgiveness can be had if there is total repentance. If there have been problems, there must be a total transformation of one's life, if he is to be forgiven.

2. Preparing one's mind and the spirit to know the truth. To arrive at mission age and be illiterate in the gospel or the common knowledge of the world would be most unfortunate indeed. Certainly by the time young people reach the age

when they are eligible to be called, they should be prepared to step from conventional roles at home into the important role of the missionary without a total reorganization of their life, standards, or training.

3. Preparing to finance the mission so it may be the missionary's own contribution, as far as is possible. It costs money to go to the various parts of the world and preach the gospel. How wonderful it would be if each future missionary were to have saved for a mission from birth. How wonderful it would be if each missionary were to totally or largely finance his or her own mission and thereby receive most of the blessings coming from missionary labors.

From whatever money comes to hand through gifts or earnings, it would be wise to set apart a portion in a savings account or safe investment to be used for a mission. Pennies make dollars, and sacrifices for a just cause make character.

Of course, if one is a convert as a teenager, the years of saving are limited. Or if the economic standards are low and opportunities are severely limited, the young person may not be able to save much, but he or she should still be governed by this policy so far as is possible and make a personal sacrifice.

Our work is to preach the gospel to the world. It is not self-imposed. We are under divine commandment. The Prophet Joseph Smith preached, "After all has been said, the greatest and most important duty is to preach the gospel." All the other programs are extremely important but, of course, we cannot influence people much by those programs until we get them in the Church.

After his resurrection the Lord took his eleven apostles to the top of the Mount of Olives and said: "And ye shall be witnesses unto me both in Jerusalem, and in all Judea, and in Samaria, and unto the uttermost part of the earth." (Acts 1:8.)

These were his last words on earth before he ascended to his heavenly home. What is the significance of the phrase "uttermost part of the earth"? He had already covered the area known to the apostles. Was it only the people in Judea? Or those in Samaria? Or the few millions in the Near East? Where were the "uttermost parts of the earth"? Did he include the hundreds of thousands or even millions in Greece, Italy, around the Mediterranean, the inhabitants of Central Europe? Did he mean the millions in what is now America? Or did he mean all the living people of all the world and those spirits assigned to this world to come in future centuries? Have we underestimated his language or its meaning? How can we be satisfied with 100,000 converts out of 4 billion people in the world who need the gospel?

The Savior said:

"All power is given unto me in heaven and in earth.

"Go ye therefore, and teach all nations, baptizing them in the name of the Father, and of the Son, and of the Holy Ghost." (Matthew 28:18-19.)

He said "all nations."

Remember, our ally is our God. He is our commander. He made the plans. He gave the commandment.

Blessings That Have Been Promised

The Lord has promised great blessings to us in proportion to how well we share the gospel. We will receive help from the other side of the veil as the spiritual miracles occur. The Lord has told us that our sins will be forgiven more readily as we bring souls unto Christ and remain steadfast in bearing testimony to the world, and surely every one of us is looking for additional help in being forgiven of our sins. (See D&C 84:61.) In one of the greatest of missionary scriptures, section 4 of the Doctrine and Covenants, we are told that if we serve the Lord in missionary service "with all [our] heart, might, mind, and strength," then we may "stand blameless before God at the last day."

Further, the Lord said: "And if it so be that you should labor all your days in crying repentance unto this people, and bring, save it be one soul unto me, how great shall be your joy with him in the kingdom of my Father!

"And now, if your joy will be great with one soul that you have brought unto me into the kingdom of my Father, how great will be your joy if you should bring many souls unto me!" (D&C 18:15-16.)

If one labors all his days and brings in save it be one soul! What joy! One soul! How precious! Oh, that God would give us that kind of love for souls!

What a marvelous opportunity our missionaries have! They are making the final preparation for their life's work. They are not going to be common men and women. Every one of them and everyone who is preparing for a mission must be special so that the Lord will approve of them and appreciate them. Today they are building their life just as much as if they had loads of gravel and stacks of timber to build it with. If we could see our lives twenty years from now, we could each go back and decide: It was back there during those years when I was preparing to be a missionary and giving missionary service that I set the direction of my life.

Do you think that the only reason the Lord has called them to the mission field is to preach the gospel? Absolutely not. That is important, but they are also called into the mission field to make sons and daughters of God into strong, powerful leaders in the future.

Your Life's Mission

A great prophet of the Lord once said to a group of missionaries: "You are being released from this mission. You have filled two years. But you are not released from your life's mission, and you never will be. Your mission is for the rest of your life, though you will receive additional and changing assignments."

You who serve a full-time mission as young adults may well live an additional sixty years or more. In those sixty years, what a powerful influence for good you can be. And you must do it! This is serious business. We are not merely inviting people to go on missions. We are saying, this is your work! The God of heaven, through his prophets, has called you to this service. Every man, woman, and child who has the gospel, who has been baptized, has a responsibility.

I have no fear whatever that the candle lighted in Jerusalem years ago will ever be put out. It will shine ever more brightly. This is the work of the Lord. We are on his errand. He has commanded us specifically, and yet we are unknown among many people of the world. It is time to gird up our loins and go forward with new dedication to this great work. We covenanted, you and I, to do it. May we all say with that young man found by his anxious parents in the temple sitting in the midst of the scholars, "I must be about my Father's business."

PRESIDENT KIMBALL
SPEAKS OUT ON
SERVICE TO OTHERS

We have been told that society in the last days would display some of the social symptoms that existed in the time of Noah. Noah's contemporaries were apparently very disobedient to the commandments of God; the earth was "corrupt," and, significantly, society then was "filled with violence." (Genesis 6:11.)

Violence and corruption usually occur because of selfishness. In a time like this, how fitting it is that we focus on service to our fellowmen! The Lord said in the Sermon on the Mount:

"Ye are the light of the world. A city that is set on an hill cannot be hid.

"Neither do men light a candle, and put it under a bushel, but on a candlestick; and it giveth light unto all that are in the house.

"Let your light so shine before men, that they may see your good works, and glorify your Father which is in heaven." (Matthew 5:14-16.)

Service to others deepens and sweetens this life while we are preparing to live in a better world. It is by serving that we learn to serve. When we are engaged in the service of our fellowmen, not only do our deeds assist them, but we also put our own problems in a fresher perspective. When we concern ourselves more with others, there is less time to be concerned with ourselves. In the midst of serving, there is the promise of Jesus that by losing ourselves, we find ourselves!

The Need for Service

The Lord does notice us, and he watches over us. But it is usually through another person that he meets our needs. Therefore, it is vital that we serve each other. The righteous life is achieved as we magnify our view of life and expand our view of others *and* of our own possibilities. Thus, the more we follow the teachings of the Master, the more enlarged our perspective becomes. We see many more possibilities for service than we would have seen without this magnification. There is great security in spirituality, and we cannot have spirituality without service!

The abundant life noted in the scriptures is the spiritual sum that is arrived at by the multiplying of our service to others and by investing our talents in service to God and to man. Jesus said, you will recall, that on the first two commandments hang all the law and the prophets, and those two commandments involve developing our love of God, of self, of our neighbors, and of all men. There can be no real abundance in life that is not connected with the keeping and the carrying out of those two great commandments.

Unless the way we live draws us closer to our Heavenly Father and to our fellowmen, there will be an enormous emptiness in our lives. It is frightening for me to see, for instance, how the life-style of so many today causes them to disengage from their families and their friends and their peers toward a heedless pursuit of pleasure or materialism. So often loyalty to family, to community, and to country is pushed aside in favor of other pursuits that are wrongly thought to be productive of happiness when, in fact, they often produce only questionable pleasure that passes quickly.

One of the differences between true joy and mere pleasure is that certain pleasures are realized only at the cost of someone else's pain. Joy, on the other hand, springs out of selflessness and service, and it benefits rather than hurts others.

Appropriate Service

Latter-day Saints everywhere are encouraged to become actively engaged in worthy causes that will improve their communities and make them more wholesome places in which to live and raise a family.

Some observers might wonder why we concern ourselves with such simple things as service to others in our communities when the world is in turmoil over wars and other dramatic problems. Yet, one of the advantages of the gospel of Jesus Christ is that it gives us perspective about the people on this planet, including ourselves. Most of us have little influence on world affairs. If we can make a contribution to peace on a large scale, we should do so; but our first task is to regulate our own lives properly and to care for our families and our neighbors before we go too far afield.

There is no end of potential causes to which you can devote your time and talents and treasure. Be careful to select good causes. There are many of these causes to which you can give yourself fully and freely and which will produce much joy and happiness for you and for those you serve. There are other causes, from time to time, that may seem more fashionable and that may produce the applause of the world, but these are often selfish in nature. These latter causes tend to arise out of what the scriptures call "the commandments of men" rather than the commandments of God. Such causes have some virtues and some usefulness, but they are not as important as those causes which grow out of keeping the commandments of God to bless the lives of the widows and orphans, the sick and the sorrowing, and to love our neighbors as ourselves.

Civic Service

Early in this dispensation the Lord made clear the position his restored church should take with respect to civil government. In a revelation he gave to the Prophet Joseph Smith, he said: "And now, verily I say unto you concerning the . . . law of the land which is constitutional, supporting that principle of freedom in maintaining rights and privileges, [that it] belongs to all mankind, and is justifiable before me. Therefore, I, the Lord, justify you . . . in befriending that law which is the constitutional law of the land." (D&C 98:4-6.)

In harmony with this statement, the Church later adopted as one of its Articles of Faith: "We believe in being subject to kings, presidents, rulers, and magistrates, in obeying, honoring, and sustaining the law." (Article of Faith 12.)

Uphold and sustain the law, and work within the law to be an influence for good, as the Prophet Joseph Smith counseled us. Seek to help select wise and good men to govern. But please avoid, even by implication, involving the Church in political issues. It is so easy, if we are not careful, to project our personal preferences as the position of the Church on an issue.

Missionary Work and Personal Example

One of the most important and rewarding ways in which we can serve our fellowmen is by living and sharing the principles of the gospel. We need to help those whom we seek to serve to know for themselves that God not only loves them, but he is also ever mindful of them and their needs. To teach our neighbors of the divinity of the gospel is a command reiterated by the Lord: "It becometh every man who hath been warned to warn his neighbor." (D&C 88:81.)

Not all of us can engage in full-time missionary

work, where one might have opportunity to explain the gospel and bear testimony of its divinity many times a day. But every member most definitely *can* follow President David O. McKay's inspired slogan, "Every member a missionary." He can befriend and fellowship nonmember neighbors, fellow employees, friends and acquaintances, and those with whom he is engaged in community service. By his interest and association, he should strive to bring those nonmembers to the point where they will willingly receive the stake or full-time missionaries. What every member ought to do, by good example and by bearing testimony, is to portray to nonmembers the joys of gospel living and understanding and thus help to bring them to the stage where they will accept more formal teaching.

The proper motivation for missionary work of any kind, as for all Church service, is, of course, love for fellowmen; but always such work has its by-product effect on one's own life. Thus, as we become instruments in God's hands in changing the lives of others, our own lives cannot help being lifted. One can hardly help another to the top of the hill without climbing there himself.

Service Brings Growth

In serving others, we "find" ourselves in terms of acknowledging divine guidance in our lives. Furthermore, the more we serve our fellowmen in appropriate ways, the more substance there is to our souls. We become more significant individuals as we serve others. We become more substantive as we serve others. Indeed, it is easier to "find" ourselves because there is so much more of us to find!

George MacDonald observed that "it is by loving and not by being loved that one can come nearest to the soul of another." (*George MacDonald Anthology,* London: Geoffrey Bles, 1970.) Of course, we all need to be loved, but we must be giving and not always receiving if we want to have a wholeness to our lives and a reinforced sense of purpose.

In the account of the barren fig tree (see Matthew 21:19) the unproductive tree was cursed for its barrenness. What a loss to the individual and to humanity if the vine does not grow, the tree does not bear fruit, the soul does not expand through service! One must live, not merely exist; he must do, not merely be; he must grow, not just stagnate. We must use our talents in behalf of our fellowmen, rather than burying them in the tomb of a self-centered life. Personal purity and veracity and stability in leadership are essential if we are to give sanctified service to others. We must expend our energies and use our skills for purposes larger than our own self-interest if we desire true happiness.

May we ponder carefully, deeply, and prayerfully our roles in life, where we can give the greatest service, to whom we can make the greatest contribution, what we should do with our lives and with our special skills and training. Our success will be measured by what we can give of our lives and our contribution to others rather than what we can get and receive from others.

The happy and abundant life begins from within and then moves outward to other individuals and to our communities. If there is richness and righteousness in us, then we can make a difference in the lives of others and in our towns, just as key individuals have influenced the lives of each of us for good and have made us richer than we otherwise would have been.

What is our greatest potential? Is it not to be Christlike ourselves? And what are the qualities we must develop to achieve such greatness? We might consider intelligence, light, knowledge, and leadership. But perhaps the most essential godlike quality is that of compassion and love—compassion shown forth in service to others, unselfishness, that ultimate expression of concern for others which we call love. Wherever our Father's children magnify their opportunities for loving service, they are learning to become more like him.

In answer to the question, "Which is the great commandment in the law?" the Savior has set our course:

"Thou shalt love the Lord thy God with all thy heart, and with all thy soul, and with all thy mind.

"This is the first great commandment.

"And the second is like unto it, Thou shalt love thy neighbour as thyself.

"On these two commandments hang all the law and the prophets." (Matthew 22:37-40.)

PRESIDENT KIMBALL
SPEAKS OUT ON
PROFANITY

In the hospital one day I was wheeled out of the operating room by an attendant who stumbled, and there issued from his angry lips vicious cursing with a combination of the names of the Savior. Even half-conscious, I recoiled and implored: "Please! Please! That is my Lord whose names you revile."

There was a deathly silence; then a subdued voice whispered, "I am sorry." He had forgotten for the moment that the Lord had forcefully commanded all his people, "Thou shalt not take the name of the Lord thy God in vain; for the Lord will not hold him guiltless that taketh his name in vain." (Exodus 20:7.)

Many people would excuse themselves for

cursing by saying that the Ten Commandments were given millennia ago to a faraway people, but it must be remembered that the Lord not only gave them with power to the Israelites, but he also reiterated them with emphasis to the Jews in the meridian of time, and even in our own dispensation he has repeated them for our own benefit and guidance.

To the young man of Jerusalem who asked the way of salvation, Christ said, "If thou wilt enter into life, keep the commandments." (Matthew 19:17.)

The eager inquirer asked, "Which?"

The Lord then repeated for him the Ten Commandments. They were still applicable. He also said in the Sermon on the Mount, "Swear not at all." (Matthew 5:34.)

Paul, the apostle, condemned profane people, saying, "Their throat is an open sepulchre; with their tongues they have used deceit; the poison of asps is under their lips: Whose mouth is full of cursing and bitterness." (Romans 3:13-14.)

And James lashed out against the evil: "But the tongue can no man tame; it is an unruly evil, full of deadly poison. . . . Out of the same mouth proceedeth blessing and cursing. My brethren, these things ought not so to be." (James 3:8, 10.)

In this latest dispensation the Lord warns, "Wherefore, let all men beware how they take my name in their lips—For behold, verily I say, that many there be who are under this condemnation, who use the name of the Lord, and use it in vain." (D&C 63:61-62.)

Yet on the corner, in public places, on work

projects, at banquet tables, there come ringing into our ears the sacred names of Deity spoken without solemnity. When we go to places of entertainment and mingle with people, we are shocked at the blasphemy that seems to be acceptable among them. It is heard on the stage, in the movies, on television, and on the radio. We understand how Lot must have felt when he was, according to Peter, "vexed with the filthy conversation of the wicked." (2 Peter 2:7.) We wonder why those of coarse and profane conversation, even if they refuse obedience to God's will, are so stunted mentally that they let their capacity to communicate grow more and more narrow.

Language is like music: we rejoice in beauty, range, and quality in both, and we are demeaned by the repetition of a few sour notes.

Profanity in Popular Literature

I recently picked up a book, widely circulated, highly recommended, a best-seller, and my blood ran cold at the profane and vulgar conversations therein, and I cringed as the characters used in an ugly way the sacred names of Deity. Why? Why do authors sell themselves so cheaply and desecrate their God-given talents? Why do they profane and curse? Why do they take in their unholy lips and run through their sacrilegious pens the names of their own Creator, the holy names of their Redeemer? Why do they ignore his positive command?

"And ye shall not swear by my name falsely, neither shalt thou profane the name of thy God: I am the Lord." (Leviticus 19:12.)

48

"Shall the axe boast itself against him that heweth therewith?" (Isaiah 10:15.)

A group of young basketball players climbed aboard a bus on which I was riding. They seemed to vie with each other to see who could curse most viciously. Perhaps they had learned it from older men as they associated with them in various activities. I know they did not fully realize the seriousness of their words.

At the beach one day a group of youths had driven their car too far out in the sand, and it was imbedded deeply. All their combined strength seemed insufficient to dislodge it. I offered to assist, but the vile language they were using repelled me. Teenagers were using the holy names of their Creator as though he were their creation. I shrank from the blasphemy and left them.

Some time ago I saw a drama enacted on the stage of a San Francisco theater. The play had enjoyed a long, continuous run in New York. It was widely heralded. But the actors, unworthy to unloose the latchets of the Lord's sandals, were blaspheming his sacred name in their common, vulgar talk. They repeated words of a playwright, words profaning the holy name of their Creator. The people laughed and applauded, and as I thought of the writer, the players, and the audience, the feeling came to me that all were party to the crime, and I remembered the castigation in Proverbs to those who condone evil:

"Whoso is partner with a thief hateth his own soul: he heareth cursing, and bewrayeth it not." (Proverbs 29:24.)

On the stage, on the telephone, sensitive ears and eyes are outraged daily by the unwarranted and blasphemous use of the names of the Lord our God. In the club, on the farm, in social circles, in business, and in every walk of life, the names of the Redeemer are used presumptuously and sinfully. We who are thoughtless and careless, and we who are vicious and defiant, should remember that we cannot with impunity take the name of the Lord in vain. Are we not inviting eventual destruction as we desecrate all things holy and sacred, even to the common and irreverent use in our daily talk of the names of Deity?

Accountable for Our Language

The Lord has told us that we are accountable for indecent language. I hope that you would not ever use any indecent language, my young friends. That would be a disgrace. Indecency that is designed to impress will only depress the hearers as well as the person who utters the indecency. If mankind could but come to see indecency as an indication of weakness and not strength and maturity, as stupidity and not sophistication, then they would come to see more clearly the strength of Jesus Christ, the most honest and decent individual who ever lived on the face of the earth.

It is a terrible thing for any human being to use the names of Deity in disrespect. Through the ages, the prophets have never ceased to rebuke this grave sin. The prophet Isaiah called to accounting and repentance those "which swear by the name of the Lord, and make mention of the

God of Israel, but not in truth, nor in righteousness." (Isaiah 48:1.)

Job, informed that his socially minded sons
and daughters were dissipating in their homes,
"offered burnt offerings according to the number
of them all; for Job said, It may be that my sons
have sinned, and cursed God in their hearts." (Job
1:5.) He was in great distress. His bones ached; his
flesh was sore; his heart was tried; and his hope
near gone. Yet when his wife rebelled, saying,
"Dost thou still retain thine integrity? curse God
and die," faithful Job reprimanded her severely:
"Thou speakest as one of the foolish women
speaketh." (Job 2:9-10.)

George Washington also set us a good example in this regard. When he learned that some of
his officers were given to profanity, he sent a
letter to them on July 1, 1776, saying: "The General is sorry to be informed that the foolish and
wicked practice of profane cursing and swearing,
a vice heretofore little known in our American
army, is growing into fashion. He hopes the
officers will, by example as well as influence, en-
deavor to check it and that both they and the men
will reflect that we can have little hope of the
blessing of heaven on our arms if we insult it by
our impropriety and folly. Added to this, it is a
vice so mean and low, without any temptation,
that every man of sense and character detests and
despises it."

Our Responsibilities as Latter-day Saints

Speaking the Lord's name with reverence
must simply be part of our lives as members of the

Church. For example, we, as good Latter-day Saints, do not smoke. We do not drink. We do not use tea and coffee. We do not use illicit drugs. By the same token, we do not use foul language. We do not curse or defame. We do not use the Lord's name in vain. It is not difficult to become perfect in avoiding a swearing habit, for if one locks his mouth against all words of cursing, he is en route to perfection in that matter.

But our responsibility does not end there. That would merely be to refrain from committing sin. To perform righteousness, we must speak our Lord's name with reverence and holiness in our prayers, our discourses, and our discussions. Isaiah sang, "For unto us a child is born, unto us a son is given; and the government shall be upon his shoulder: and his name shall be called Wonderful, Counseller, the mighty God, The everlasting Father, The Prince of Peace." (Isaiah 9:6.)

Jesus perfected his life and became our Christ. Priceless blood of a God was shed, and he became our Savior; his perfected life was given, and he became our Redeemer; his atonement for us made possible our return to our Heavenly Father, and yet how thoughtless, how unappreciative are most beneficiaries! Ingratitude is a sin of the ages.

Great numbers profess belief in him and his works, and yet relatively few honor him. Millions call themselves Christians, yet seldom kneel in gratitude for his supreme gift, his life.

Let us rededicate ourselves to reverential attitudes, toward an expression of gratitude to our Lord for his incomparable sacrifice. Let us remember the modern command, "Wherefore, let all men beware how they take my name in their lips." (D&C 63:61.)

PRESIDENT KIMBALL
SPEAKS OUT ON
PERSONAL JOURNALS

On a number of occasions I have encouraged the Saints to keep personal journals and family records. I renew that admonition. We may think there is little of interest or importance in what we personally say or do, but it is remarkable how many of our families, as we pass on down the line, are interested in all that we do and all that we say.

Any Latter-day Saint family that has searched genealogical and historical records has fervently wished its ancestors had kept better and more complete records. On the other hand, some families possess some spiritual treasures because ancestors have recorded the events surrounding their conversion to the gospel and other happenings of interest, including many miraculous blessings and spiritual experiences.

People often use the excuse that their lives are uneventful and nobody would be interested in what they have done. But I promise you that if you will keep your journals and records and write your personal histories, they will indeed be a source of great inspiration to your families, your children, your grandchildren, and others, on through the generations. Each of us is important to those who are near and dear to us—and as our posterity read of our life's experiences, they too will come to know and love us. And in that glorious day when our families are together in the eternities, we will already be acquainted.

Would that every family, as they now hold their home evenings, would train their children from young childhood to keep a journal of the important activities of their lives, certainly by the time they begin to leave home for schooling and missions.

From time immemorial the Lord has counseled us to be a record-keeping people. Abraham had a book of remembrance, and Adam had one. You may think of them as not being as highly educated as we are, but they were well-trained people. Adam spent much effort being the school teacher for his children. He and Eve taught their sons and daughters. He taught them the gospel in their home evenings, and he taught them reading and writing and arithmetic. And they kept their books of remembrance. How else do you think Moses, many hundreds of years later, got the information he compiled in the book of Genesis?

These records had been kept, and he referred to them and got the history of the world, which wasn't in any library other than that. Can you see your responsibility?

Records from the Past

Early in the American life of the family of Lehi, his son Nephi said: "Having had a great knowledge of the goodness and mysteries of God, therefore, I make a record of my proceedings in my days. . . . And I know that the record which I make is true; and I make it with mine own hand; and I make it according to my knowledge." (1 Nephi 1:1, 3.) This great record included not only the movements of his people, but also his own personal life.

When the Savior visited this continent following his resurrection, he commanded the Nephites and Lamanites to bring their records up to date. He said to them: "Behold, other scriptures I would that ye should write, that ye have not.

"And it came to pass that he said unto Nephi: Bring forth the record which ye have kept.

"And when Nephi had brought forth the records, and laid them before him, he cast his eyes upon them and said:

"Verily I say unto you, I commanded my servant Samuel, the Lamanite, that he should testify unto this people, that at the day that the Father should glorify his name in me that there were many saints who should arise from the dead, and should appear unto many, and should minister unto them. And he said unto them: Was it not so?

"And his disciples answered him and said: Yea, Lord. . . .

"And Jesus said unto them: How be it that ye have not written this thing, that many saints did arise and appear unto many and did minister unto them?

"And it came to pass that Nephi remembered that this thing had not been written, . . . therefore it was written according as he commanded." (3 Nephi 23:6-13.)

I am glad that it was not I who was reprimanded, even though mildly and kindly, for not having fulfilled the obligation to write the records and keep them up to date.

Again, in our day the Lord said to the Prophet Joseph Smith, "And again, let all the records be had in order, that they may be put in the archives of my holy temple." (D&C 127:9.)

Your Own Journal

You should continue on in this important work of recording the things you do, the things you say, the things you think, to be in accordance with the instructions of the Lord. Your story should be written now while it is fresh and while the true details are available.

Your private journal should record the way you face up to challenges that beset you. Do not suppose life changes so much that your experiences will not be interesting to your posterity. Experiences of work, relations with people, and an awareness of the rightness and wrongness of actions will always be relevant. Your journal, like most others, will tell of problems as old as the world and how you dealt with them.

Your journal should contain your true self rather than a picture of you when you are "made up" for a public performance. There is a temptation to paint one's virtues in rich color and whitewash the vices, but there is also the opposite pitfall of accentuating the negative. Personally I have little respect for anyone who delves into the ugly phases of the life he is portraying, whether it be his own or another's. The truth should be told, but we should not emphasize the negative. Even a long life full of inspiring experiences can be brought to the dust by one ugly story. Why dwell on that one ugly truth about someone whose life has been largely circumspect?

Your journal contains the raw materials for your personal history or autobiography, so it should be kept carefully. You are unique, and there may be incidents in your experience that are more noble and praiseworthy in their way than those recorded in any other life.

What could you do better for your children and your children's children than to draw upon your journal to write the story of your life, your triumphs over adversity, your recovery after a fall, your progress when all seemed black, your rejoicing when you finally achieved? Some of what you write may be humdrum, but there will also be rich passages that will be quoted by your posterity.

We hope you will begin as of this date. If you have not already commenced this important duty in your lives, get a good notebook, a good book that will last through time and into eternity for the angels to look upon. Begin today and write in it your goings and your comings, your deeper thoughts, your achievements and your failures, your associations and your triumphs, your impressions and your testimonies.

We hope you will do this, our brothers and sisters, for this is what the Lord has commanded, and those who keep a personal journal are more likely to keep the Lord in remembrance in their daily lives.

PRESIDENT KIMBALL
SPEAKS OUT ON
TITHING

In times of troublous economic concern and worry, we must forcefully remind ourselves, both individually and as a church, that the Lord has given us a spiritual and economic law that, when fully obeyed, will bring promised blessings so great that "there will not be room enough to receive" them. (Malachi 3:10.)

I speak of the law of tithing, which can be our great blessing and safety, our great assurance of divine assistance. It has always been impressive to me that of all the teachings from Old Testament prophets that the Lord could have given anew to the Nephites when he visited them, he gave Malachi's stirring promise regarding tithing:

"And it came to pass that [Jesus] commanded

them that they should write the words which the Father had given unto Malachi, which he should tell unto them. And it came to pass that after they were written he expounded them. And these are the words which he did tell unto them, saying: Thus said the Father unto Malachi . . . Will a man rob God? Yet ye have robbed me. But ye say: Wherein have we robbed thee? In tithes and offerings.

"Ye are cursed with a curse, for ye have robbed me, even this whole nation.

"Bring ye all the tithes into the storehouse, that there may be meat in my house; and prove me now herewith, saith the Lord of Hosts, if I will not open you the windows of heaven, and pour you out a blessing that there shall not be room enough to receive it.

"And I will rebuke the devourer for your sakes, and he shall not destroy the fruits of your ground; neither shall your vine cast her fruit before the time in the fields, saith the Lord of Hosts.

"And all nations shall call you blessed." (3 Nephi 24:1, 8-12.)

Who in our time does not need these promised blessings?

The Lord Prospers Judah

In hard times once were another people, the people of the kingdom of Judah. They had lived through the wickedness of King Ahaz; they had suffered economic and political reverses at the hands of the Assyrians and Philistines. But when young King Hezekiah began to reign, "he did that which was right in the sight of the Lord." (2

Chronicles 29:2.) Thus, the hearts and minds of the people were again turned to the teachings of the scriptures, and the commandments were again followed. The story of what happened thereafter is another witness of how the Lord fulfills his promises:

"And as soon as the commandment came abroad, the children of Israel brought in abundance the firstfruits of corn, wine, and oil, and honey, and of all the increase of the field; and the tithe of all things brought they in abundantly.

". . . they also brought in the tithe of oxen and sheep, and the tithes of holy things which were consecrated unto the Lord their God, and laid them by heaps. . . .

"And when Hezekiah and the princes came and saw the heaps, they blessed the Lord, and his people Israel.

"Then Hezekiah questioned with the priests and the Levites concerning the heaps.

"And Azariah the chief priest of the house of Zadok answered him and said, Since the people began to bring the offerings into the house of the Lord, we have had enough to eat, and have left plenty: for the Lord hath blessed his people; and that which is left is this great store. . . .

"And thus did Hezekiah throughout all Judah, and wrought that which was good and right and truth before the Lord his God.

"And in every work that he began in the service of the house of God, and in the law, and in the commandments, to seek his God, he did it with all his heart, and prospered." (2 Chronicles 31:5-6, 8-10, 20-21.)

The Lord prospered Judah through their hard times because it truly is as the Psalmist says: "The earth is the Lord's, and the fulness thereof; the world, and they that dwell therein." (Psalm 24:1.)

Promises in the Latter Days

In the latter days the Lord has said that if the Saints keep the commandments and "offer [their] oblations," "the fulness of the earth is [theirs], the beasts of the field and the fowls of the air. . . . Yea, all things which come of the earth . . . are made for the benefit and use of man." (D&C 59:12, 16, 18.)

The prophets of all dispensations have clearly taught the law of tithing for the blessing and protection of the Lord's people. On this subject, we may read the word of the Lord in our dispensation:

"Verily, thus saith the Lord, I require . . . that, those who have thus been tithed shall pay one-tenth of all their interest annually; and this shall be a standing law unto them forever, for my holy priesthood, saith the Lord. . . .

"And I say unto you, if my people observe not this law, to keep it holy, and by this law sanctify the land of Zion unto me, that my statutes and my judgments may be kept thereon, that it may be most holy, behold, verily I say unto you, it shall not be a land of Zion unto you.

"And this shall be an ensample unto all the stakes of Zion. Even so. Amen." (D&C 119:1, 4, 6-7.)

The Lord herein makes clear that tithing is his law and is required of all his followers. It is our honor and privilege, our safety and promise, our great blessing to live this law of God. To fail to meet this obligation in full is to deny ourselves the promises and to omit a weighty matter. It is a transgression, not an inconsequential oversight.

Yes, it may take great faith to pay tithes when funds are scarce and demands are great. But we remember the promise from the Father to Malachi. We also remember the Lord's promise in our day: "I, the Lord, am bound when ye do what I say; but when ye do not what I say, ye have no promise." (D&C 82:10.)

These principles should be taught with regularity and with living testimony by parents to their children. The time to teach these real lessons of life is when the child is small. As a child he is receptive, he is open, and he will accept the suggestions of his parents.

Lessons Learned in Youth

I remember as a youth walking with my mother up the dusty road to the bishop's house in a day when we often paid tithing from our animals and produce. As we walked, I said, "Why do we take the eggs to the bishop?" She answered, "Because they are tithing eggs, and the bishop receives the tithing for Heavenly Father." My mother then recounted how each evening when the eggs were brought in, the first one went into a small basket and the next nine went into a large basket. I first learned the law of tithing from my beloved mother.

To the west of our home was our garden plot. Part of the garden was in potatoes. One day my father said to my sister and me, "There are more potatoes than we can use. If you would like to sell some, you may do so."

My sister Alice and I dug some up and hauled them down to a hotel and sold them. When we showed the money to our father, he asked what we were going to do with it. We said we would divide it before buying some things we wanted. Then he questioned, "What about your tithing?" He said, "The Lord has been good to us. We planted and cultivated and harvested, but the earth is the Lord's. He sent the moisture and the sunshine. One-tenth we always give back to the Lord for his part."

My father made no requirement; he merely explained it so convincingly that we felt it an honor and privilege to pay tithing.

"The Earth Is the Lord's . . ."

Years ago I had a friend who took me to his ranch. He unlocked the door of a large new automobile, slid behind the wheel, and said proudly, "How do you like my new car?" We rode in luxurious comfort into the rural areas to a beautiful new landscaped home, and he said with no little pride, "This is my home."

He drove to a grassy knoll. The sun was setting behind the distant hills. He surveyed his vast domain. Pointing to the north, he asked, "Do you see that clump of trees?" I could plainly discern it in the fading day.

He pointed to the east. "Do you see the lake shimmering in the sunset?" It too was visible.

"Now, the bluff that's on the south." We

turned about to scan the distance. He identified barns, silos, the ranch house to the west. With a wide, sweeping gesture, he boasted, "From the clump of trees to the lake, to the bluff, and to the ranch buildings and all between—all this is mine. And the dark specks in the meadow—those cattle are also mine."

And then I asked from whom he obtained it. The chain of title of his abstract went back to land grants from governments. His attorney had assured him he had an unencumbered title.

"From whom did the government get it?" I asked. "What was paid for it?" There came into my mind the declaration of the Psalmist, boldly restated by Paul: "The earth is the Lord's, and the fulness thereof." (1 Corinthians 10:26.)

And then I asked, "Did title come from God, Creator of the earth and the owner thereof? Did he get paid? Was it sold or leased or given to you? If a gift, from whom? If a sale, with what exchange or currency? If a lease, do you make proper accounting? What was the price? With what treasures did you buy this farm?"

"Money!"

"Where did you get the money?"

"From my toil, my sweat, my labor, and my strength."

And then I asked, "Where did you get your strength to toil, your power to labor, your glands to sweat?"

He spoke of food.

"Where did the food originate?"

"From sun and atmosphere and soil and water."

"And who brought those elements here?"

I quoted the Psalmist: "Thou, O God, didst send a plentiful rain, whereby thou didst confirm thine inheritance, when it was weary." (Psalm 68:9.)

"If the land is not yours," I said, "what accounting do you make to your landlord for his bounties? The scripture says: 'Render therefore unto Caesar the things which are Caesar's; and unto God the things that are God's.' (Matthew 22:21.) What percentage of your increase do you pay Caesar? And what percent to God?

"Do you believe the Bible? Do you accept the command of the Lord through the prophet Malachi? Do you believe Moses' words to Pharaoh that 'the earth is the Lord's'?" (Exodus 9:29.)

I said again: "I seem to find no place in holy writ where God has said, 'I give you title to this land unconditionally.' I cannot find such scripture, but I do find this from the Psalms: 'Those that wait upon the Lord, . . . shall inherit the earth.' (Psalm 37:9.)

"And I remember that our Creator covenanted in the council in heaven with us all: 'We will go down, for there is space there, and we will take of these materials, and we will make an earth whereon these may dwell.' (Abraham 3:24.) It seems more of a lease on which a rental is exacted than of a simple title. This does not seem to convey the earth, but only the use and contents, which are given to men on condition that they live all of the commandments of God."

However, my friend continued to mumble, "Mine—mine," as if to convince himself against the surer knowledge that he was at best a recreant renter.

That was long years ago. I later saw him lying in his death among luxurious furnishings in a palatial home. His had been a vast estate. And I folded his arms upon his breast and drew down the little curtains over his eyes. I spoke at his funeral, and I followed the cortege from the good piece of earth he had claimed to his grave, a tiny, oblong area the length of a tall man, the width of a heavy one.

Later I saw that same estate, yellow in grain, green in lucerne, white in cotton, seemingly unmindful of him who had claimed it.

A Great Blessing and a Law

My dear brethren and sisters, I testify to all of you that tithing is indeed a great blessing and a law for our benefit. Let us again read the promise that came from the Father, a promise none of us can afford to be without: "Bring ye all the tithes into the storehouse, that there may be meat in mine house, and prove me now herewith, saith the Lord of Hosts, if I will not open you the windows of heaven, and pour you out a blessing that there shall not be room enough to receive it." (Malachi 3:10.)

Let this, then, be our watchword: "As for me and my house, we will serve the Lord." (Joshua 24:15.)

If we will do so, and keep the commandments with all our heart as did Hezekiah, the Lord will guide us through troublous times, and we shall gratefully see his help in our behalf, and we will give deep love and appreciation to him for his many kindnesses and goodnesses. He is our Lord and our great strength. If we are worthy, he will be there in our time of need. Of that I have a sure understanding.

PRESIDENT KIMBALL
SPEAKS OUT ON
ADMINISTRATION TO THE SICK

W e believe in the gift of tongues, prophecy, revelations, visions, healing. . . ." (Article of Faith 7.) As the Savior sent out his apostles to proselytize the world after his ascension, he gave them this commission:

"Go ye into all the world, and preach the gospel to every creature.

"He that believeth and is baptized shall be saved; but he that believeth not shall be damned.

"And these signs shall follow them that believe; In my name shall they cast out devils; they shall speak with new tongues;

" . . . and if they drink any deadly thing, it shall not hurt them; *they shall lay hands on the sick, and they shall recover.*" (Mark 16:15-18. Italics added.)

The Lord was promulgating an eternal principle that where his priesthood is and where faith is found, there will be the signs of power—not for show, but for a blessing to the people. This eternal principle was understood by the disciples of the Lord in early days. James said:

"Is any sick among you? let him call for the elders of the church; and let them pray over him, anointing him with oil in the name of the Lord:

"And the prayer of faith shall save the sick, and the Lord shall raise him up. . . .

". . . The effectual prayer of a righteous man availeth much." (James 5:14-16.)

When John the Baptist, languishing in prison, sent messengers to the Lord to inquire, "Art thou he that should come or do we look for another?" (Matthew 11:3), the Lord's answer relayed back was, "Go and shew John again those things which ye do hear and see: The blind receive their sight, and the lame walk, the lepers are cleansed, and the deaf hear, the dead are raised up, and the poor have the gospel preached to them." (Matthew 11:4-5.)

In his commission to the seventies, whom he sent out into every city and place whither he himself would come, he gave the commission to "heal the sick that are therein, and say unto them, The kingdom of God is come nigh unto you." (Luke 10:9.)

And when the seventy returned again with joy, saying, "Lord, even the devils are subject unto us through thy name," the Savior said:

"I beheld Satan as lightning fall from heaven.

"Behold, I give unto you power to tread on serpents and scorpions, and over all the power of the enemy: and nothing shall by any means hurt you.

"Notwithstanding in this rejoice not, that the spirits are subject unto you; but rather rejoice, because your names are written in heaven." (Luke 10:18-20.)

"And they cast out many devils, and anointed with oil many that were sick, and healed them." (Mark 6:13.)

The use of oil in administration and blessing seems to have been a practice from earliest times. Jacob poured oil on the stone he used for a pillow when he had spiritual manifestations. Oil was used in the anointing of kings. When Saul was called by the Lord to be king over Israel, he was anointed by Samuel of the tribe of Benjamin. He "was a choice young man, and a goodly: and there was not among the children of Israel a goodlier person than he: from his shoulders and upward he was higher than any of the people. . . .

"Now the Lord had told Samuel in his ear a day before Saul came, saying, . . . thou shalt anoint him to be captain over my people Israel, that he may save my people out of the hand of the Philistines: for I have looked upon my people, because their cry is come unto me. And when Samuel saw Saul, the Lord said unto him, Behold the man whom I spake to thee of! this same shall reign over my people." (1 Samuel 9:2, 15-17.)

Samuel sent Saul to the high place to eat with him and promised to answer the query in his mind and heart concerning the whereabouts of the lost asses Saul was seeking. When they came down from the high place of the sacrifice, Samuel accompanied Saul on his way; and when they were at the edge of the city, the servant was allowed to proceed, but Saul was kept back to hear the "word of God."

"Then Samuel took a vial of oil, and poured it upon his head, and kissed him, and said, Is it not because the Lord hath anointed thee to be captain over this inheritance?

"And the Spirit of the Lord will come upon thee, and thou shalt prophesy with them [the company of prophets], and shalt be turned into another man.

"And it was so, that when he had turned his back to go from Samuel, God gave him another heart." (1 Samuel 10:1, 6, 9. Italics added.)

In the famous 23rd Psalm the use of oil is indicated: "Thou anointest my head with oil; my cup runneth over." (Psalm 23:5.)

The use of oil in healings was mentioned many times, but not always. Whether or not oil was used in those cases is not known, but the custom and practice are established. Blessings may be given with or without oil.

The Anointing and the Sealing

Administration to the sick is an ordinance of two parts—the anointing and the sealing. An elder pours a small quantity of oil on the head of the one to be blessed, near the crown of the head if convenient, never on the other parts of the body, and in the name of the Lord and by the authority of the priesthood, he anoints the person for the restoration of health. The sealing is performed by two or more elders, one of whom, as mouth, seals the anointing and gives an appropriate blessing, also in the name of Jesus Christ and by authority of the priesthood.

Sometimes when oil is not available, or when two brethren are not present, or when the sick one has recently been anointed, a substitute program is followed whereby one or more elders give a blessing, likewise in the name of the Lord and by authority of the Melchizedek Priesthood. He will pronounce such blessings as seem appropriate and as the Spirit moves.

Anyone may pray for the sick; this is not a priesthood ordinance. Such a prayer of faith makes request to the Lord to heal, whereas the blessing or the administration is given by the power of the priesthood and in the name of Christ.

I feel that sometimes the holy ordinance is abused. One person I know left a standing order for the elders to administer to her every day for the several weeks she was in the hospital for a broken limb. Many feel that too frequent administrations may be an indication of lack of faith or of the ill person trying to pass the responsibility for faith development to the elders rather than self.

I learned a valuable lesson once long ago from a sweet lady, Sister Lucy Grant Cannon, who became violently ill while visiting her daughter in Arizona. We elders were promptly called, and we administered to her. The next day she was asked if she wished to be administered to again and her reply was, "No, I have been anointed and administered to. The ordinance has been performed. It is up to me now to claim my blessing through my faith."

Sometimes when one still feels the need of further blessing after having recently had an administration, a blessing without the anointing oil is given.

The need for faith is often underestimated. The ill person and the family often seem to depend wholly on the power of the priesthood and the gift of healing that they hope the administering brethren may have, whereas the greater responsibility is with him who is blessed. There are persons who seem to have the gift to heal, as indicated in Doctrine and Covenants, section 47, and it is understandable why a sick one might desire a blessing at the hands of a person who seems to have great faith and proven power, and in whom the recipient has confidence, but the major element is the faith of the individual when that person is conscious and accountable. "Thy faith hath made thee whole" was repeated so often by the Master that it almost became a chorus. Though he was the Redeemer and "all power is given [him] in heaven and in earth," yet his oft-repeated statement was, "Thy faith hath made thee whole." "As with your faith, so shall it be unto you."

The centurion approached the Lord in Capernaum and appealed for restoration to health of his grievously tormented servant at home. He said, "I am not worthy that thou shouldest come under my roof: but speak the word only, and my servant shall be healed." He likened the spiritual power of Christ to his own military power.

Christ, astonished, said: "I have not found so great faith, no, not in Israel. . . . Go thy way; and

75

as thou hast believed, so be it done unto thee. And his servant was healed the selfsame hour." (Matthew 8:8, 10, 13.)

There is the woman whose serious affliction had continued twelve years; she pleaded, "If I may but touch his garment I shall be whole." She touched the hem of his garment and recovered from that hour: "Daughter, be of good comfort; thy faith hath made thee whole." (Matthew 9:21-22.)

And again, in the land of Gennesaret all who were afflicted touched the hem of his garment and all were healed, "made perfectly whole." (See Matthew 14:35-36.)

Blind Bartimaeus also received his sight after his persistent, faithful efforts to reach the Lord. And as sight came to the man of Jericho, the Lord said: "Thy faith hath made thee whole." (See Mark 10:46-52.)

A seeing man became an ardent follower. "According to your faith be it unto you." (Matthew 9:29.) The Lord said to the two other blind men whose eyes he touched and healed, "Believe ye that I am able to do this?" (Matthew 9:28.) And two more blind persons could see.

The Canaanite woman, willing to accept the crumbs of the blessings, was rewarded in the restoration of her afflicted daughter when the Redeemer promised, "O woman, great is thy faith: be it unto you even as thou wilt." (Matthew 15:28.)

When the Lord saw the monumental faith of the palsied man whose friends made a hole in the roof and lowered the sick man on his bed through the aperture to the feet of the Lord, who was speaking to a full house, the Lord said, "Son, be of good cheer; thy sins be forgiven thee," and the sick one walked forth, carrying his bed. How could such faith go unrewarded? (Matthew 9:2. See also Mark 2:1-5.)

Those Who May Perform Blessings

Because individuals have preferences, it is sometimes found that certain officials are besieged constantly to give blessings. When one is ill and weak and terrified, it is natural to want elders in whom he has much confidence because of their righteous living and their proven faith and devotion. It should be remembered, however, that not just the General Authorities or the stake or ward or mission authorities have the priesthood with power to heal. Numerous brethren throughout the Church, including home teachers, have the authority to bless; and their administration or blessing, combined with great faith from the blessed one, can bring about spectacular healings. This is evidenced by the numerous wonderful healings brought about through the ministrations of young, inexperienced missonaries.

Wondering or skeptical people often ask, Why are there not the spiritual manifestations today, including healings, as in the days of the Prophet Joseph Smith and the days of the Savior?

The answer is clear: There are infinitely more healings today than in any age, and they are just as wondrous. The religious history of the Savior's ministry and the period following is written in a few short chapters; as John said, "There are also many other things which Jesus did, the which, if they should be written every one, I suppose that even the world itself could not contain the books that should be written." (John 21:25.)

As the history of the years was condensed, it would be expected that only the most spectacular of the healings would be chronicled, giving the impression that all miracles were spectacular ones and that all who asked were healed. Little mention is made of the possibly numerous times in Christ's and the later apostles' ministries when the blessings were not so outstanding, when a headache was stopped, when a recovery was greatly speeded up, or when agonies were relieved. Today the libraries would bulge their walls if all the miracles of our own time were recorded.

When I toured the European missions in 1955, I heard the testimonies of hundreds of missionaries. In many there were repeated stories of miracles, astounding in their performance. For instance, there were many who told of serious operations required by the medical profession for serious maladies. The times were set for surgery, and after administration and prayer and fasting, the same doctors came forth with new X rays to say that something had happened and the surgery was not necessary. It happened so many times that it could hardly be a fanatic interpretation or a zealot imagining things. All of them could not have been imagined or misinterpreted or fancied. Such cancelled operations have been reported in many countries by missionaries from many hometowns in different times and at widely separated places and under different circumstances to many people at home and abroad.

Instantaneous healings are numerous. They range into the areas of sight, hearing, lameness, internal organs, skin, bones, and all parts of the body. Incurable diseases have been healed. We are grateful beyond expression for the great skill and accumulated knowledge and patience and understanding possessed by our physicians. But it must be that numerous healings credited to doctors and hospitals have been the healing of the Lord through the priesthood and by prayer. We are generally too ready to give the credit to the physician when at best his was but a contribution, small or large.

It must be remembered that no physician can heal. He can only provide a satisfactory environment and situation so that the body may use its own God-given power of re-creation to build itself. Bones can be straightened, germs can be killed, sutures can close wounds, and skillful fingers can open and close bodies; but no man yet has found a way to actually heal. Man is the offspring of God and has within him the re-creating power that is God-given. And through the priesthood and through prayer, the body's healing processes can be speeded and encouraged.

There are many who run to the doctor first and then go later to the elders when all other hope is gone. Elders are often called to the hospital to administer after the medical profession has done all it can. Then when the ill person is on his way to recovery, his recovery is credited to the scientist;

or in the case of death, some wonder why the priesthood did not heal him. But whether the Lord sees fit to heal instantaneously or gradually, whether it be through surgery and treatment or without it, the healing is still the Lord's miracle. While the medical profession has worked hard to gain the accumulated knowledge of today, we must remember that He who created our bodies has known since the beginning how to remodel, re-create, and repair bodies.

When elders bless and recoveries do not follow, frequently there is not only disappointment but also sometimes a diminishing of faith, especially where there have also been many prayers and long fastings. The Lord has told us, " . . . if they die they shall die unto me, and if they live they shall live unto me." (D&C 42:44.)

Again, it must be remembered that not all the sick and afflicted were healed in other dispensations either. Even the first great Apostles asked, "Why could we not cast him out?" And the answer from the Lord seemed not too condemnatory. "This kind goeth not out but by fasting and prayer." (Matthew 17:19, 21.)

Though Peter and his associates performed numerous miracles, many of which are recorded for us, even to the raising of the dead, it is known that they did not heal all who desired restoration. Even the Savior, with all power on earth and in heaven, did not heal them all. He could have done so, that is certain, but many did not have the faith to be healed. In his own world of Nazareth he performed few of his miracles. He was the boy from Nazareth, without honor in his own home town.

80

"He did not many mighty works there because of their unbelief." (Matthew 13:57-58.) Others he did not heal probably because they were not to be healed.

An Appointed Time to Die

Death is a part of life. People must die. There can never be total victory over disease and death until the end of time. Much headway has been made, and mortality tables are encouraging; more infants survive, more mothers go through childbirth successfully, and more people, generally, live to a riper age than in centuries past. We are grateful to all those hard-working scientists who have contributed to this great accomplishment. But die we must; otherwise there could be no resurrection, and without that there could be no immortality and further development. We seem to be rapidly changing our mode of dying from the sickbed to the street, or the ditch, or the canyon in traffic accidents. But die we must.

Naturally we all properly postpone our deaths as long as possible, but the day must come. To pray for or bless even the very aged or the seemingly incurable still seems proper, for we do not know the times appointed nor when one should return to the next world. So we pray and bless consistent with the mind and will of the Lord, who does know the end from the beginning and who can heal if it is right. But it is not likely that there will be a healing if the appointed time to die has come.

There have been exceptions, however, when the time has been postponed. Notable among

81

these is the case of King Hezekiah, who pled for an extension period and who was granted fifteen years, after which he moved on. Many times, in our own experience, it would seem that there may have been time extensions granted through monumental faith. Thoughtful folks must realize, however, that there often comes a time when it is imprudent to demand an extension of the Lord and most unsound to ask in an unqualified manner for an extension. Sometimes such could be a boomerang that would prolong, unwarrantedly, the time of suffering and deprivation and, in some cases, the burden upon the family. Consequently our prayers are properly offered and blessings pronounced if there is not an unqualified demand for restoration. Sometimes the body, under such circumstances, neither lives nor dies.

It seems to me that until our wisdom and judgment catch up with the latent power we hold, we must be extremely careful in telling the Lord what he must do. Perhaps no one would ever die if we had our way.

Occasionally people become overly sentimental and fanatic, and ascribe as a miracle everything that happens. But for every person who is overzealous or who is overpsychic or fanatical, there are numerous persons who fail to see the miracle in numerous healings. "They would have recovered anyway," they say. I give one example:

The Lord said to his own, "O ye of little faith." Aren't we all? Once when I was far away from home, after three days of quite intense suffering, I finally admitted to my companion, Brother Harold B. Lee, that I was in distress. He gave me a sleeping pill he had with him, then knelt by my bed and blessed me. Though I had gone through three nights in pain and almost without sleep (it was then three o'clock in the morning), I was fast asleep moments after the blessing. I am now ashamed to confess that the next morning when I awakened, my first thought was of the potency of the pill. Then, as hours passed and I knew the effect of the pill must have passed, the distress did not return, and I fell on my knees in remorse to ask forgiveness of the Lord for my having given credit to the medicine rather than to him. Months passed and still there was no return of pain or distress. I am ashamed, but I probably represent numerous people who have done likewise.

As I went into surgery a few years ago, I was still conscious when the doctors and nurses were standing around me. I said to the specialist, "There are numerous people full of faith who are praying for you this morning." He quietly replied, "I'll need their prayers." The skeptic may have another answer, but it is my firm conviction that the numerous prayers were heard, that his hand was steadied and guided, that his judgment increased, and that as a result of the blessings of the Lord, healing followed and voice returned to a satisfactory extent.

"See Thou Tell No Man"

Sometimes I have cringed to hear elders tell of miracles in which they were the administrators. It has sounded like boasting, reminding me of the Lord's caution to the triumphant seventies: "Notwithstanding in this rejoice not, that the spirits are subject unto you; but rather rejoice, because your names are written in heaven." (Luke 10:20.)

I would fear to boast of miracles in which I was part for fear the Lord might be displeased even to the extent of curtailing his power entrusted to me.

The blessing belongs to the recipient, who may wish properly to bear testimony to it; but it would seem ill fitting and presumptuous to even approach boasting, for none of us can heal. Only by the priesthood are results manifested. If an elder were to charge the afflicted one never to mention those who laid on hands, it would further take away the temptation to take honors unto oneself. All honor should be given our Heavenly Father. Such a procedure seems to be in line with the Savior's life, for in many healings he charged, "Tell no man." To the leper asking mercy he said, "I will, be thou clean," and immediately the leprosy was cleansed. Then Jesus said, "See thou tell no man." (Matthew 8:3-4.)

I know that the healing power is in the Church and that numerous people are healed or improved or restored through the blessings of the Lord, sometimes with and sometimes without the skill of men.

We should do all we can for ourselves first: through proper diet, rest, and applying common sense, especially for minor trouble. Then we may send for the elders, the home teachers, or the neighbors or friends in whom we have confidence. Frequently this is all that is required, and numerous healings can be effected. In serious cases where the problem is not solved, we should turn to those who can help so wonderfully. One young woman who was sent to the hospital for serious surgery, and who was jittery with fear, stated that when the doctor came to see her the night before the early morning surgery, he indicated he had been to the temple. She relaxed and felt at peace, realizing that she was in the hands of a righteous, skilled man of faith, and that the Lord was watching.

Let not the skeptic disturb your faith in miraculous healings. They are numerous. They are sacred. Many volumes would not hold them. They are simple and also complex. They are both gradual and instantaneous. They are a reality.

PRESIDENT KIMBALL
SPEAKS OUT ON
PLANNING YOUR LIFE

Youth, beloved youth, what a world you live in! What glorious opportunities are yours!

For the first decade of your life there were joyous, happy, irresponsible days. Your parents and family protected you, taught and fed you, clothed and sheltered you; but now in the second decade of your life there is some relaxation of control. Gradually you are developing your personality, making increased numbers of your own decisions. You are maturing and assuming responsibility. The most important decisions of your entire life are before you—decisions that can open up for you glorious, progressive pathways, or send you into dismal, dead-end streets.

. Others can help you toward your decisions, but you must make them and you must abide by them. Free agency gives you the right to choose, but it gives you no immunity from the deprivation and sufferings that wrong decisions bring. Once you have set your feet upon the highway of life, the turning is not easy, especially if that highway be filled with heavy traffic and if it be a downward road.

Your life is your own, to develop or to destroy. You can blame others little and yourself almost totally if that life is not a productive, worthy, full, and abundant one. Others can assist or hinder you, but the responsibility is yours, and you can make it great, mediocre, or a failure.

I grew up in a dry country. It seemed to me that hardly ever was there enough rain to spread over the crop-growing period to carry us through the season—not enough water to distribute between the many hungry canals and the tens of thousands of thirsty acres, not enough to irrigate all the crops. We learned to pray for rain—we always prayed for rain.

The Need for Reservoirs

When I was still very small, I knew that plants could not survive in dry country more than about two or three weeks without water. I knew how to harness up the old mare to a lizard (a forked log on which a barrel was placed), and I drove the animal to the "big ditch," the Union Canal, which was a block below our home. With a bucket I scooped up water from the small stream or the puddles and filled the barrel; and the horse dragged it back so I could pour bucketfuls of precious liquid on the roses, the violets, and the other flowers, and the small shrubs and hedges and new trees. Water was like liquid gold, so reservoirs became the warp and woof of the fabric of my life.

In our times there is a need for reservoirs of many kinds—reservoirs to store water; some to store food, as we do in our family welfare program; some like the barns and bins set up by Joseph in the land of Egypt, in which the people stored the seven years of plenty to carry them over the seven years of drought and famine.

There should also be reservoirs of knowledge to meet future needs; reservoirs of courage to overcome the floods of fear that put uncertainty in lives; storage of physical strength to help us meet the frequent contaminations and contagions; reservoirs of goodness; reservoirs of stamina; reservoirs of faith. Yes, reservoirs of faith so that when the world presses in upon us, we stand firm and strong. When the temptations of a decaying world about us draw on our energies, sap our spiritual vitality, and seek to pull us down to the level of the worldly world, we need a storage of faith that can carry youth through the tantalizing teens and through the problems of later years, faith to carry us over the dull, the difficult, the terrifying moments, over disappointments, disillusionments, and years of adversity, want, confusion, and frustration.

How do we fill our reservoirs?

As a keenly observant generation of Latter-day Saints, it must be clear to you by now that you live in times filled with perplexity and difficulty, but these are times which are also filled with great opportunity.

I am grateful that you and all of us have the gospel of Jesus Christ as a guide, so that we have a framework of understanding into which we can fit the events and circumstances that we will live to see. It is clear from the scriptures that we in this part of our dispensation cannot be promised by our political leaders that there will be "peace in our time," but we, as church members, are given the means of having a personal peace, of coming to know serenity in our souls—even when there is no peace without!

By now you are perhaps accustomed to having those of us who are further along the pathway of life describe to you the importance of staying on the "strait and narrow" path. So often we say many of the same things to you again and again, but if you reflect upon why that is so, you will soon discover that the precipices that lie on each side of that narrow path don't change or become less dangerous; the steepness of that path does not change.

Church leaders are not able, each time we teach you, to offer a new or more glamorous route that will lead back to the presence of our Heavenly Father. The route remains the same. Hence, encouragement must often be given concerning the same things and warnings must be repeated. Just because a truth is repeated does not make that truth any less important or true. Indeed, the opposite is true.

"The glory of God is intelligence, or, in other words, light and truth" (D&C 93:36), say the modern revelations, and "pure knowledge . . . shall greatly enlarge the soul" (D&C 121:42).

We read also, "It is impossible for a man to be saved in ignorance." (D&C 131:6.) This is greatly misunderstood. Without waiting to find out the true meaning, many young people jump at conclusions and go off unprepared, following the traffic without road maps, and end in disappointment.

Knowledge of God and Secular Learning

In what kind of ignorance is the danger of damnation? In what kind of knowledge is found power, and what power comes from knowledge? Let us analyze this great truth. In proper sequence, first comes the knowledge of God and his program, which is the way to eternal life, and then comes the knowledge of the secular things, which is also very important. The Creator himself gives the proper sequence and defines the order: "Seek ye first the kingdom of God, and his righteousness; and all these things shall be added unto you." (Matthew 6:33.) And through Joseph Smith he says: "This is eternal lives—to know the only wise and true God, and Jesus Christ, whom he hath sent. I am he. Receive ye, therefore, my law." (D&C 132:24.)

Now this mortal life is the time to prepare to meet God, which is our first responsibility. Having already obtained our bodies, which become the permanent tabernacles for our spirits through the eternities, now we are to train our bodies, our minds, and our spirits. Preeminent, then, is our using this life to perfect ourselves, to subjugate

the flesh, to subject the body to the spirit, to overcome all weaknesses, to govern self so that one
may give leadership to others, and to perform all
necessary ordinances. Second comes the preparation for the subduing of the earth and all the elements. We have this life of limited years in which
to learn of God and to become the masters of our
own destiny; we have in addition this life plus
eternities to learn of the earth and the things
thereon, and to accumulate secular knowledge
that will help make us gods, which is our destiny.

Peter and John had little secular learning, being termed ignorant. But they knew the vital
things of life, that God lives and that the crucified,
resurrected Lord is the Son of God. They knew
the path to eternal life. This they learned in a few
decades of their mortal life. Their righteous lives
opened the door to godhood for them and creation of worlds with eternal increase. For this they
would probably need, eventually, a total knowledge of the sciences. But whereas Peter and John
had only decades to learn and do the spiritual,
they have already had nineteen centuries in
which to learn the secular or the geology of the
earth, the zoology and physiology and psychol-
ogy of the creatures of the earth. Mortality is the
time to learn first of God and the gospel and to
perform the ordinances. After our feet are set
firmly on the path to eternal life we can amass
more knowledge of the secular things.

The so-called ignorant Peter and John are heirs
to exaltation and can learn what they need to
know to create worlds. A highly trained scientist
who is also a perfected man may create a world

and people it, but a dissolute, unrepentant, unbelieving one will never be such a creator even in the eternities.

Secular knowledge, important as it may be, can never save a soul nor open the celestial kingdom nor create a world nor make a man a god, but it can be most helpful to that man who, placing first things first, has found the way to eternal life and who can now bring into play all knowledge to be his tool and servant.

Challenge to Read the Scriptures

Once I heard a forceful appeal by a woman from the Mutual. Perhaps it was the approach she made or perhaps it was the mood I was in. She gave a rousing talk on the reading of the scriptures and making them our own; then she stopped her dissertation to ask this mixed congregation, about a thousand of us, "How many of you have read the Bible through?"

I think I was about fourteen years old at the time. An accusing guilt complex spread over me. I had read many books by that time, the funny papers, and light books, but my accusing heart said to me, "You, Spencer Kimball, you have never read that holy book. Why?" I looked around me at the people in front and on both sides of the hall to see if I was alone in my failure to read the sacred book. Of the thousand people, there were perhaps a half dozen who proudly raised their hands. I slumped down in my seat. I had no thought for the others who had also failed, but only a deep, accusing thought for myself. I don't know what other people were doing and thinking, but I heard no more of the sermon. It had accomplished its work. When the meeting closed, I sought the large double exit door and rushed to my home a block east of the chapel; and I was gritting my teeth and saying to myself, "I will. I will. I will."

Entering the back door of our family home, I went to the kitchen shelf where we kept the coal oil lamps, selected one that was full of oil and had a newly trimmed wick, and climbed the stairs to my attic room. There I opened my Bible and began on Genesis, first chapter and first verse, and I read well into the night with Adam and Eve and Cain and Abel, and Enoch and Noah and through the flood even to Abraham.

Learning the things of God must include, of course, the even more difficult part—that of becoming the perfected being. You must not only avoid adultery, but you must also protect yourself against every thought or act that could lead to such a terrible sin. You must not only be free from revenge and retaliation, but you must also "turn the other cheek," "go the second mile," "give the cloak and coat also." You must not only love friends, but you must love even your enemies and those who do you injustice; you must pray for them and actually love them. This is the way to perfection. You must not only be above burglary or theft, but you must also be honest in thought and deed in all the numerous areas where rationalization might permit dishonesty—in padding reports, in chiseling on time or money or labor, and in every shady or questionable practice. You must not only cease from your worship of things of wood and stone and metal, but you must also actively worship in true fashion the living God. This is the "strait and narrow" way.

Now may I make a recommendation? Develop discipline of self so that, more and more, you do not have to decide and redecide what you will do when you are confronted with the same temptation time and time again. You need only to decide some things once. How great a blessing it is to be free of agonizing over and over again regarding a temptation. To do such is time-consuming and very risky.

Likewise, my dear young friends, the positive things you will want to accomplish need be decided upon only once—like going on a mission and living worthily in order to get married in the temple—and then all other decisions related to these goals can fall into line. Otherwise, each consideration is risky, and each equivocation may result in error. There are some things Latter-day Saints do and other things we just don't do. The sooner you take a stand, the taller you will be!

From my infancy I had heard the Word of Wisdom stories about tea and coffee and tobacco, etc. Nearly every Sunday School day and Primary day we sang lustily, I with the other boys:

> *That the children may live long,*
> *And be beautiful and strong,*
> *Tea and coffee and tobacco they despise,*
> *Drink no liquor, and they eat*
> *But a very little meat;*
> *They are seeking to be great and good and wise.*

We sang it time and time again until it became an established part of my vocabulary and my song themes, but more especially my life's plan. Occasionally some respected speaker said he had never tasted the forbidden things we sang against and then I made up my mind. Never would I use these forbidden things the prophets preached against. That decision was firm and unalterable. I would not and did not deviate.

In 1937 my wife and I were touring in Europe. In France I sat at a banquet table of the Rotary International convention in a fashionable hotel. The large, spacious banquet room held hundreds of people. The many waiters moved about the tables, and at every place besides plenteous silver, linen, and fancy serving dishes were seven wine glasses. No one was watching me. The temptation nudged me: Shall I drink it or at least sip it? No one who cares will know. Here was quite a temptation. Shall I or shall I not?

Then the thought came: I had made a firm resolution as a boy that I would never touch the forbidden things. I had already lived a third of a century firm and resolute. I would not break my record now.

"Wickedness Never Was Happiness"

Remember, O youth of a noble birthright, that "wickedness never was happiness." The unrighteous may pretend to be happy and may seek to entice others into such a way of life because misery loves company, as you know, but you will never see a happy sinner. Even the discontent of good people is traceable to such shortcomings as they may have.

A casual observer may feel that an unrighteous person "has it made," and for a fleeting moment it may even seem so. But gross sin produces deep emptiness. Thus the wicked seem to do more of the same in order to reassure themselves and to try to fill the void. When you see a life filled with desperation, there is transgression in it. We may pity such people, but it is wrong and naive to envy them!

To know the patriarchs and prophets of the ages past and their faithfulness under stress and temptation and persecution strengthens the resolves of youth. All through the scriptures almost every weakness and every strength of man has been portrayed, and rewards and punishments have been recorded. One would surely be blind who could not learn to live life properly by such reading. The Lord has said, "Search the scriptures, for in them ye think ye have eternal life: and they are they which testify of me." (John 5:39.)

He is the same Lord and Master in whose life we find every quality we should develop in our own lives.

Can you find in all the holy scriptures where the Lord Jesus Christ ever failed his church? Can you find any scripture that says he was untrue to his people, to his neighbors, his friends, or his associates? Was he faithful? Was he true? Is there anything good and worthy that he did not give? Then that is what we ask—what he asks of a husband, every husband: of a wife, every wife; of a girl, every girl; of a boy, every boy.

Another word of counsel as you plan the course of your life: To do the special things given to this generation, you will need to guard against selfishness. One of the tendencies most individuals have that simply must be overcome is the tendency to be selfish. All that you can do now while you are young and are more pliant to become less selfish and more selfless will be an important and lasting contribution to the quality of your life in the years, indeed in the eternity, to come. You will be a much better wife or a much better husband, a better mother or a better father, if you can curb the tendency to be selfish. Your children, whom you will not know for a few years yet, have a stake in your conquest of selfishness.

As in all things, we have the example of the Savior on the cross at Calvary. He did something that he was not forced to do—something that would benefit others with the gift of immortality that Jesus already had. His was the supreme act of selflessness.

You may recall reading in 3 Nephi about the visit of the resurrected Jesus to the American continent and how after blessing the children he wept twice and said, "And now behold, my joy is full." (3 Nephi 17:20.)

True joy can come only from giving ourselves to correct causes such as the building up of the kingdom, causes that are in a sense larger than we are. Pleasure tends to be self-centered. True joy always includes others.

Now is the time to set your life's goals. Now is the time to set your standards firmly and then hold to them throughout your life.

Ernest Renon once said: "Everything favors those who have a special destiny; they become glorious by a sort of invincible impulse and command of fate."

Your Special Destiny

I see in you, my young friends, a generation of Latter-day Saints rising up who will be much more familiar with the scriptures than previous generations of Latter-day Saints were at the same age. You can be lifelong students of the scriptures.

I see in you a rising generation of young Latter-day Saints who will be more willing to do missionary work (both before and after your formal full-time missions) than previous generations. Speaking collectively, your generation will see, even more clearly than your predecessors, how important it is to take the gospel to your fellowmen. Your generation will be unashamed of the gospel of Jesus Christ and equally unashamed of The Church of Jesus Christ of Latter-day Saints.

I see in you a generation of young Latter-day Saints whose hearts will be turned to your forefathers as has never before happened on such a scale. You will develop a natural interest in research and temple going, surpassing the interest levels in this regard of your parents and grandparents when they were your age.

I see in you a generation of young Latter-day Saints who will make effective use of your leadership experiences gained in the Church in the Young Men and Young Women programs, in Sunday School, in Relief Society, in Primary, and in the priesthood quorums, who will then be sought after by the thoughtful people of the world who will want young men and women of integrity and competency to serve in various ways.

I see in you a generation of young Latter-day Saints with testimonies much more advanced for your age than those of preceding generations.

And so, beloved youth, remember, when the temporal kingdoms of men topple, the kingdom of God stands firm and unshaken. When the earthly influence of the worldly-wise is silenced by death, the glory and progress of the faithful and valiant who have lived all requirements live on in majesty and power. There is no other way.

INDEX

Abandonment of sin, 13-14
Accountability for language, 50
Administration to sick: described in scriptures, 70-73; under unusual circumstances, 74; abuse of, 74; without anointing, 74, 75; numerous brethren have authority for, 77; not always efficacious, 80
Anointing of sick, 73-74

Banquet in France, 95
Barren fig tree, 44
Bible, Spencer W. Kimball decided to read, 92-93
Boasting in healings, 83-84

Cannon, Lucy Grant, 74
Causes, select good, 41
Chastity, law of, 9-10
Children of God, we are, 2
Church, don't involve in issues, 42
Civil service encouraged, 41-42
Confession of sin, 14-15
Couple who committed fornication, 3-5

Death, 81-82
Decisions, 94
Doctors, 79, 85
Do the will of the Father, 16-17

Earth is the Lord's, 65-68
Evil is widespread, 3

Faithful, all should be, 96
Forgiveness for immorality not easy to obtain, 6
Fornication condemned, 8-9
Friendship not courtship, 9-10

Gospel: to be preached in all the world, 29, 34; teachings of, repeated, 89
Growth through service, 43-45

Healings: by Savior, 71; through prayer, 74; depend on faith, 75-77; through faith, examples of, 75-77; numerous, exist today, 77-79; related by missionaries, 78-79; man not responsible for, 79; do not always take place, 80; not always appropriate, 82; many do not believe in, 82; do not boast of, 83-84; testimony of, 84-85
Health, how to preserve, 84
Hezekiah, King, 61-63, 82
Homosexuality, 10-12
Hopes, anchor to God, 26
Hospital attendant who used profanity, 46

Immorality begins with small indiscretions, 5
Incest, 6
Issues, don't involve Church in, 42

Jesus Christ was true and faithful, 96
Journals: importance of keeping, 54-55; of interest to posterity, 54-55; kept by Adam, 55-56; how to keep, 57-59
Joy: and pleasure, 40; through selflessness, 98
Judah, kingdom of, prospered through tithing, 61-63

Kimball, Spencer W.: testimony of, 26-27; paid tithing on potatoes, 64-65; blessed by Harold B. Lee, 82-83; hauled water, 87-88; decided to read Bible, 92-93; decided to keep Word of Wisdom, 94-95; at banquet, 95
Knowledge, 90-92

Language is like music, 48
Last days are like time of Noah, 38

101